"In this remarkable book, Will Pye sho[...] [...radical, transformative power of] gratitude. Moving far beyond clichéd 's[...] [...] ences with brain cancer to reveal the [...] in even the worst possible situations. [...] both practical suggestions and effecti[...] [...] honest, encouraging, and warmhearted voice. A lovely, important book."

—**Rick Hanson, PhD**, author of *Just One Thing* and *Resilient*

"Copious scientific evidence links gratitude to greater happiness, as well as mental and physical health. But the 'how' of milking gratitude for its medicinal properties is often vague. Fortunately, *The Gratitude Prescription* is just what the doctor ordered. Overflowing with practical, actionable gratitude practices, those who want to optimize their thankfulness for the purposes of healing and happiness can now follow their intuition in choosing among the many tools this book offers. How do we know if we can trust this guidance? Because Will Pye writes from direct experience. As a man who found a way to be grateful for even his brain tumor as part of his journey to cure, you can bet there's no better teacher of radical gratitude."

—**Lissa Rankin, MD**, *New York Times* bestselling author of *Mind Over Medicine* and *The Daily Flame*

"As always with Will Pye's work, *The Gratitude Prescription* starts with a simple but powerful premise before taking the reader on a ride deep into what it means to a human being who is alive, whole, and transformed."

—**Nick Jankel**, founder of the transformation company Switch On, and author of *Spiritual Atheist*

"In this extraordinary book, Will Pye guides readers through a rich journey of deep healing and transformation. Simple yet impactful exercises illuminate the power of gratitude both for well-being and for supporting realization of your inherent unity consciousness. Along with Will's inspiring story and life-changing insights, his book paves the way for readers to directly experience their innate happiness and what it means to be and live fully alive."

—**Carole Griggs, PhD**, author of *Space to See Reality*, cofounder of iConscious™, and professor of conscious human development at John F. Kennedy University

"*The Gratitude Prescription* is an exquisite blend of scientific and spiritual truths, inspiring readers to explore for themselves the practical wisdom of radical gratitude. Truly a timely and much-needed resource."

—**Linda Graham, MFT**, author of *Bouncing Back* and *Resilience*

"What does it mean to be fully human? This is the question that Will Pye's brilliant new book explores. His own experiences with a brain tumor, and the profound mystical states it enables him to access, are presented here, but in a manner that allows us to follow along. Deeply experiential in its orientation, Will doesn't ask us to take anything he says on faith. Instead he guides us through exercises and meditations designed to show us a deeper view of ourselves and our world—for ourselves. Bolstered by cutting-edge brain science, developmental psychology, and physics, even skeptics will come to understand why gratitude and love are what Will's long and profound journey have left him holding, as the two greatest ways we can live as human beings."

—**Keith Martin-Smith**, award-winning author of
A Heart Blown Open and *Only Everything*

"Resting on a foundation of gratitude, Will Pye beckons us back home to who we really are at our essence—being, breath, and awareness. Who we are is so much bigger than any experience we have or circumstance we find ourselves in. Will helps us reconnect to the profound simplicity of our being—to the Love that we are—and find everything we need to navigate the ups and downs of this journey called Life. Thank you, Will Pye."

—**Alan Seale**, director of the Center for Transformational Presence,
and author of *Transformational Presence*

"Will Pye's message is so simple, but it is also uncompromising and strong: See what happens if you are grateful…for everything. Really? Yep! The whole bittersweet journey. Love it all. After reading this beautiful book it feels the natural thing to do, and that's a life-changing realization."

—**Tim Freke**, best-selling author of *Deep Awake* and *Soul Story*

The
Gratitude
Prescription

Harnessing the Power of
Thankfulness for
Healing and Happiness

WILL PYE

REVEAL PRESS

AN IMPRINT OF NEW HARBINGER PUBLICATIONS

Publisher's Note

This publication is designed to provide accurate and authoritative information in regard to the subject matter covered. It is sold with the understanding that the publisher is not engaged in rendering psychological, financial, legal, or other professional services. If expert assistance or counseling is needed, the services of a competent professional should be sought.

Distributed in Canada by Raincoast Books

Copyright © 2019 by Will Pye
     Reveal Press
     An imprint of New Harbinger Publications, Inc.
     5674 Shattuck Avenue
     Oakland, CA 94609
     www.newharbinger.com

Cover design by Amy Shoup; Interior design by Michele Waters-Kermes; Acquired by Ryan Buresh; Edited by Melanie Bell

All Rights Reserved

Library of Congress Cataloging-in-Publication Data on file

21 20 19

10 9 8 7 6 5 4 3 2 1   First Printing

Contents

Part 4: Gratitude Reveals Truths of Existence

Introduction: Prescription

In essence, regardless of the shape that life takes before us, there is only ever one thing happening. It is your true nature, the source of wholeness and well-being. Beyond all ideas including those of good and bad, it is within, beyond, and unites this world of duality.

This book is designed to support the realization of the healed, happy being that you already are. It will guide you in cultivating thankfulness that encompasses your fragmented parts, your despair, your sadness, and your shame. In doing this, you'll encounter wholeness.

This book invites you to awaken your power of inner alchemy. It's your superpower—the ability to consciously wield attention, choose meaning, and transform shit into gold. You can bring soothing light into the darkness and allow loving presence to transmute your pain. This book is a guide to cease suffering by loving suffering, discover freedom, and be the change you wish to see in the world.

There is a part of you, present now, that is at peace, joyful, content. It is grateful for all experience, no matter the nature—painful or pleasurable. It is who you truly are. This book is about remembering what we are, for the fun of it! This precious human life is of such importance. We benefit from remembering to infuse it with joy, play, curiosity, and laughter at every opportunity. Gratitude helps such infusion immensely.

I am grateful for this book finding you and for you reading it. I trust that your experience of reading it will give rise to similar feelings of appreciation. I feel gratitude for the possibility that it may just change your life and the lives of people around you for the better.

By way of an introduction, let's begin with a question. What do a bitter and traumatic family breakup, addiction, bouts of suicidal depression, an ever-breaking heart at a world gone mad, grand mal seizures, financial loss, and brain cancer have in common?

I have found they are all great opportunities for growth and service. I have discovered that gratitude both cured any suffering I've experienced and allowed the resolution and opportunity contained within these challenges to be found immediately.

This is indicative of the potential power of gratitude. If you allow it, and play along wholeheartedly, it will change your mind, change your brain, and transform your world. Mastering gratitude allows our flourishing not in spite of life's intensity and challenge but because of them.

For life is surely intense!

Being human hurts. Birth is for many a deeply painful experience. After nine months or so of easing into having a body, cell by cell, we plunge into a world quite unlike anything we have seen. Having been connected to all the nourishment we need, we experience the pain of separation, the trauma of disconnection.

If we are lucky, we have loving parents. Even here, we will early on experience the pain of that love being withdrawn when Mom is momentarily irritated or when Dad is on a call and cannot give his full attention. We experience the pain of separation again and again.

We may experience outright abuse—physical, sexual, emotional—perhaps from one claiming to be a representative of "God" or our primary caregiver.

If our grandmother could not deal with her daughter's anger and reacted to it, we will likely suffer the same reactions from her when we get angry. If our grandfather could not handle his son's sadness, or was ashamed of his shame, we will likely in turn experience our father's discomfort with our own sadness or shame. Further to the likelihood that our parents will internalize and pass on their parenting, research has suggested that trauma of our ancestors might be passed on genetically. Rachel Yehuda's study with descendants of Holocaust survivors appears to indicate that we inherit trauma (Yehuda et al. 2016). Yehuda and her team's latest epigenetic results reveal that descendants of Holocaust survivors have different stress hormone profiles than their peers, perhaps predisposing them to anxiety disorders. Similar conclusions are drawn with studies involving children of mothers who were exposed to the World Trade Center attacks during pregnancy (Yehuda et al. 2005). There is much debate around how to interpret these studies, yet the theory that we inherit our parents' challenges, whether via internalized parenting style, the stories they tell us, or an epigenetic effect, appears to be sound.

Even if we are fortunate enough to go to a good school, to get a good education in a nurturing environment, we may experience the pain of rejection, anger, or hostility when our teachers experience moments of pain they cannot handle. We will likely face rejection from our peers or mild bullying.

As childhood fades, we are flung into the torment of our teenage years. Often no ritual nor rite of passage exists for being placed in a group of people we have never met and having to learn how to get along, how to be liked, and how to cope when we are not.

We are put through the discomfort of being presented with narratives of the world that seem insane. Yet, if Mom and Dad say that we are a sinner, that we are just a random piece of biology, or that our best bet is to make a lot of money, get a house and a family, and wait until this horrible thing called death comes, we will likely believe them.

We may experience the existential pain of living a narrative, an entire life, that we discover is entirely untrue. Put simply, we may inherit an especially partial worldview and live through/from it until we discover a more complete, up-to-date worldview.

Even if we are lucky enough to be told we can do anything we want to do, that life is full of opportunities, and we are raised in an environment where it is easy to see this is true, we will suffer failure. We will likely suffer from depression, anxiety, or both at some point in our life.

The pains stored in our body from earlier experiences, from our ancestors, will insist on being experienced. The pain of being in a world full of so much unnecessary suffering, so much insane policy, so much greed and life-poisoning madness will be felt.

We fall in love and experience the pain of loss or rejection. Even if we fall in love once and stay together for a lifetime, we will face the loss of the one we love or the knowledge that the one we love will face being alone.

If we have children, we get to experience all their pain and suffering as our own. We may experience the heartbreak of a child dying.

We may have the experience at some point of it all seeming simply too much and suicide seeming to be the only way out—in my work facilitating groups and coaching and through candid conversations with friends, this impulse is rather more common than we might like to think. Indeed, in our atomized, disconnected Western culture, we observe large numbers of people choosing to act on this impulse.

We will get sick, or someone we love will get sick.

We may live a good life, have the family, the career, yet be stuck with a deep feeling of dissatisfaction, a sense there must be something more, a gnawing feeling of this, or of ourselves, not being enough. We might gain everything we ever desired yet still experience a subtle but complete dissatisfaction, listlessness, and purposelessness.

Whatever we do or do not experience, we will face death. Life is intense.

Being human hurts.

This book is about cultivating the resilience, the peace, and the love available throughout the human experience. It is about learning to dance with life, to surf the inevitable waves, and to leverage the difficulty, the challenge, the dissatisfaction, the intensity, for expansion and well-being, for ourselves and our community. This book is about thriving, not in spite of life's difficulties but because of them.

This book is designed to support your realization that all is well, that what you are is unbreakable, that what you are is love, loved, and loving. It contains teachings and exercises to get you in touch with this truth experientially. Some of these exercises have an audio version that you can download at http://www.newharbinger.com/42020 so you can engage with them by listening in addition to reading.

I hope to support your experiencing that there is nothing—no rejection, no death, no global cataclysm, not even fear itself—to fear. May this book help you realize your true nature and the love that flows from this clarity.

Consider for a moment the possibility, however ludicrous it may seem, that everything that has ever happened, is happening, or will ever happen is but a lovingly designed part of a process with this realization as its purpose. Consider the possibility that the purpose of your life is to realize what you are, to awaken, to grow and evolve, and that everything can be alchemized for this purpose through gratitude.

By the time we have completed journeying together in these pages, it is my deepest intention that you will have tasted this truth for yourself. I will share a little of how this truth was realized for me to guide your own realization.

We will explore a key ingredient in this alchemical wizardry, an ingredient which, when applied liberally, consistently, and courageously, can turn shame into self-love, dissatisfaction into deep contentment, tumult into peace, challenge into opportunity, perceived separation into realized unity, and suffering into a balm that dissolves the bindings of being human and allows a metamorphosis into being divine beyond belief. This ingredient can turn an intensely painful life as burden into an intensely joyful life as dance and thrilling adventure.

This ingredient is gratitude. Together we will learn what gratitude is and how it is a powerful catalyst for creating healing and uncovering happiness. We will explore how it informs a way of being that is a powerfully authentic response to all circumstances, including the many challenges we collectively face. Paradoxically, this way of being with all that is, just as it is, changes everything.

If this book's heart, essence, and practical application could be captured in two words, they would be simply, "Thank you." With this in mind, and to keep it in yours, at each chapter's completion you will read "Thank you." This is to all what they seek to find. It may be one or all of the following: an expression of my appreciation that you have picked up this book and read this chapter, giving your time and attention so generously; a thanks to the opening of the heart or the shift in consciousness that your engaging with the material facilitates; a reminder of and invitation to the recognition of the presence we share; or an opportunity to once again, and again, feel the transformative power of what the 13th century mystic Meister Eckhart described as the one and only prayer you need ever offer:

Thank you.

PART 1

Gratitude's Many Powers

Chapter 1

Taste the Positivity

I used to believe that I was a terrible human being, a real idiot. At the slightest error, I would say to myself, "You fu*#ing idiot," as an affirmation-like reaction. This thought felt horrible and was clearly dysfunctional. I lived up to this self-image: I made decisions and acted accordingly, creating a vicious circle of idiotic choices and reinforced self-criticism. It was only when I began meditating, and cultivating the spacious awareness within, that I even became aware of this self-dialogue. In becoming aware of this self-image, I saw how out of congruency it was with my desire to be a kind and positive influence. I realized that I would never talk to anyone else that way and resolved to be kinder and more forgiving to myself too.

I had been so negative in my view of myself that suicide had seemed a natural and justifiable course of action. If I was worthless and without value, then ending myself made sense. Following a particularly intense bout of depression in my early twenties, I got as far as researching methods and drafting a note I would leave for my family to spare them suffering. Thankfully, I realized no matter how the letter was worded, they would suffer immensely and so I ruled out this option. I decided to live rather than commit suicide and to transform my mind and life. Part of this transformation was a year spent telling myself a different story about who I am and what the world is. I created myself anew each day by dwelling on the positive qualities of who I am through a journaling practice. I would write a paragraph or two of "I am..." listing positive attributes already present and others I wanted to embody. I would sometimes type out particularly strong versions to refer back to. Yet, to keep it creative and fresh, I started anew each day. What was the result? Gratitude for who I was and who I was becoming. Gratitude for developing more helpful beliefs about myself and the nature of the world I lived in. Behavior and action flowed from these blossoming beliefs, creating a positive self-fulfilling prophecy and neurological feedback loop. Gratitude was a powerful and effective remedy for depression. Along with exercise, the journaling process above, meditation, and learning how to feel my emotional pain through surrender, gratitude was key in solving the problem of depression.

So, when I was diagnosed with brain cancer, I also real-ized I had options about how I would view it. I could believe it was the worst thing to ever happen. However, I realized my self-diagnosis was causative and thus chose carefully. I could focus my attention on the very terrible things that might, or might not, unfold. How would that make me feel? Pretty lousy. Stressed, fearful, and in a state of dis-ease. But fortunately, I realized that this mind-set would create sickened conditions in my biochemistry that would support the creation of what I feared.

I could focus on the impossible-to-pronounce long words the doctors used in their diagnoses and see what statistical indicator this offered on survival. Instead, I realized and chose to believe the diagnosis was a continuation of my life's journey, of growth, of opportunity. I was fortunate to be able to hear and proclaim a deeper, absolute truth. This is the diagnosis I gave myself. I printed and laminated it, and I referred to it frequently, far more than the doctors' reports:

The brain tumor was a gift from Spirit. In healing my brain and life, I deepened my insight into healing, transformation, and awakening such that I now serve others in their healing, transformation, and awakening.

How did that make me feel? I got excited, felt joyful, surrendered, trusted, and felt as if I were in perfect health.

So was getting brain cancer the worst thing that ever happened to me or the best? When it rains, do we bemoan getting wet or perceive an opportunity to dance in the miracle of precipitation as the recycling of oceans, the fluid in our bodies, every tear we've ever cried? In the same way, we can perceive a depressed feeling as cause for depression or as an opportunity to feel more fully, so that our joys are greater too, and to love all parts of ourselves so much that we can know the experience of being fully, wholly loved.

Affirmation: *"Life is what I say it is, so I choose positivity."*

In Buddhism, "heaven" and "hell" can describe human states of consciousness. There is a Zen teaching that says there's not even a hair's breadth between heaven and hell. Indeed, in my experience they are complementary: it is necessary to experience intense suffering and dysfunction, disconnection and despair, fear and self-loathing to know—and be able to choose—contentment and purposeful thriving, connection and joy, trusting and self-loving. They are, like all opposites in duality, mutually dependent.

A key insight of our postmodern world is that truth is relative, dependent on perception and frames of reference like language, culture, and history. Yet, as we'll dive into later in the book, this is itself an absolute statement that points to the paradoxical nature of reality. Just as quantum physics has demonstrated that an electron is not a particle or a wave but both/neither, or simply a probability, we can discover through our own experience that any circumstance is seen in an infinite number of ways. The glass is both half full and half empty. The perspective we choose to take is true, so far as we believe it. It's true, real, and valid that the glass is half full and that the glass is half empty. Truth is relative; it is what we say it is.

When thoughts of terrible things, feelings of hopelessness, and reactions from fearfulness do arise, are these feelings wrong and to be avoided? Is failing to respond mindfully, consciously, and intentionally evidence that we're bad people? Naturally, negative thoughts and feelings will arise. When met positively through loving acceptance, with a willingness to feel and be present, the whole experience becomes less negative and more positive. We suddenly have an opportunity to feel more deeply, to integrate, to heal, to become more conscious. Each moment, we are given the opportunity to revise our view. This hints at the alchemical power of gratitude.

A more helpful question than "Is it true?" is "How does it make me feel?" We can feel which point of view is most beneficial. This helps us take a step into a powerful role: as creator of our circumstances, rather than victim, we can observe that there are infinite meanings and choose those that support our well-being. I encourage you to adopt this gentle attitude as you practice the meditations and exercises in this book. There is no failure, no getting it wrong. Just as any moment of exercise supports fitness, regardless of how far short we might fall of a particular goal, any moment of practice is a success. Be grateful for the ongoing learning; each misstep is an integral part of this.

Meditation: Tuning In to How Worldviews Feel

How we view the world is creative. Our fundamental beliefs about ourselves and the world we live in are causative, and affect us deeply, but we don't take the time to tune in to what feelings result. This meditation can help point out the creative effects of your worldview so that you can glimpse your creative power.

Let's start with one popular belief: "This world is a purposeless, meaningless, biological accident of physicality in which we are all in competition in a dog-eat-dog experience of lack and insufficiency that just ends in death." After reading that view, check in with how you feel. Simply notice everything that arises. It might help to put down the book and close your eyes.

What emotions arise?

Scan your body, starting with your toes and inching upward toward your head. How does your body respond? Are certain places tight, cramped, tingling, or even painful?

Do any thoughts arise, and if so, what are they?

What are you tempted to get up and do?

What becomes possible, and what becomes impossible, within this view?

Now here's an alternative view: "This world is an illusory expression of one consciousness, infinitely abundant, experiencing itself subjectively as you and me in order to know itself through an eternal and deathless exploration of love, creation, beauty, and unity."

How does that feel? Regardless of what you believe deep down, agree with, or resist, check in with how you feel. Again, put down the book, close your eyes, and simply notice.

How do you respond emotionally, physically, and mentally?

How does this view inspire you to act?

What becomes possible, and what becomes impossible, within this view?

In your journal, identify what you believe about yourself and the world. Then do the same check-in to perceive how it makes you feel. What kind of reality are you living in? Is it aligned with how you want to feel about life? Perhaps you've chosen a negative experience, or a positive one, or even abdicated your power as a creator. Take a deep breath and open to the possibility of resetting your view so that your experience can be more positive.

Be Positively Changed

I encourage you to apply the insights gained through the exercise above to your idea of who you are and what kind of world we live in, because beliefs and feelings are the scaffolding with which you create your life. It was shocking to me when doctors told me that my attitude would not affect my cancer. If I believed that, having cancer would have turned out to be as devastating as they predicted. We will always face negative views, and we can either take them on or empower ourselves by checking in with how those views make us feel. Does the view support you? If not, what does support you?

When we choose positivity, the cascading effects are vast and scientifically proven. In 1975, Harvard physician Herbert Benson (2000) described "the relaxation response" in which we intentionally trigger a very different biochemical response from the fight-or-flight survival response. We can cultivate our bodies to release chemicals and brain signals that slow responses in our muscles and organs and increase blood flow to our brain. There are many methods for doing this, including meditation, yoga, deep-breathing exercises, and focusing our attention on visualizations, sounds, or affirmations, or simply noticing our chest rise and fall when we breathe. Underlying all these efforts, and what I discovered when I was diagnosed with brain cancer, is that when we accept the world and feel positive about it, we relax when stressors and painful events come along. Most importantly these capacities of resilience can be cultivated, and gratitude is foundational.

Voluminous scientific evidence proves the causative effect of thoughts, emotions, feelings, and beliefs on our health. The placebo effect, so well established and documented, shows that even when a treatment has no active therapeutic properties, we can still experience beneficial effects because of our belief in it. Psychoneuroimmunology is the study of interactions between our minds and our nervous and immune systems. It has gathered plenty of data to conclude that bolstering our psyche supports physical health and healing.

The best news, as far as I'm concerned, comes from neuroscience. It turns out that our brains are not hardwired—they can be trained and even rewired. With this "neuroplasticity," we can mold our brains with our minds. It works like exercising. When we train our bodies regularly, we become fit to the point that even when we reduce exercise due to a change of circumstances, our bodies have been trained to continue functioning at a higher level. Neuroplasticity tells us the same is true for our brains. By building up core strengths, like gratitude, we will find ourselves with some peace and happiness in reserve for stressful times. We become more resilient.

Exercise: Linking Positivity with Gratitude

To experience the connection between gratitude and positivity for yourself, find a comfortable spot with pen and paper, and take a deep breath or two. Notice how you feel and rate your mood on a scale of 1 to 10 with 0 being miserable despair and 10 being ecstatic bliss. Write down the number. Set the timer on your phone for ten minutes.

List aspects of your life that you are grateful for beginning with "I am grateful for…" Allow your mind to flow from one item to another. Here's an example: *I am grateful for trees, the beauty they offer, the stability they teach, and the shade they provide. I am grateful for my eyesight that allows me to see all the beauty around me. I am grateful for beauty itself, in its myriad forms, and for that beautiful classical guitar music I was listening to this morning.*

After ten minutes of writing, once again take a deep breath and check in with how you are feeling. Again, rate your mood. What do you notice? What has changed? Has the rating reflected more positivity?

You can amplify the effect by doing this exercise for thirty minutes. For a truly indulgent experience, you can combine the above process with a trip to wilderness and there, rather than writing, sing, shout, or proclaim all you are grateful for. I recall one wet and windy day on a deserted New Zealand beach where after forty-five minutes of shouting aloud the beauty and brilliance of my life, I felt such exhilaration and joy that my sodden clothes and chilled body were entirely disregarded. If a reserved Englishman can do this, anyone can!

This practice will allow your mind to open to perceiving the full beauty and abundance of your life. You can do this exercise in any quiet moment you can grab, even when you can't write things down. Just run through items in your head or list ten of them on your phone with the notes function. Then you can email or text those notes to yourself, reinvigorating feelings of gratitude later, and also amass a number of notes that you can refer to over time.

Remember that any narrative or meaning you make is "true." There are infinite ways you can perceive yourself, as saint or sinner, and your life, as burden or gift, and they are all equally valid and true. When you apply this exercise to your daily life, you become ever more conscious of which story you are in. From this awareness, you can choose gratitude, again and again, to tell a story that feels good. Focus on seeing yourself and your life in a way that feels good. Focus on appreciating yourself and your life.

Change Your Brain by Making Gratitude a Habit

When you do this practice regularly over time, you will transform your brain to feel more grateful and therefore more positive. Each time you choose to feel grateful, you're "working out" this part of the brain and making it easier next time. Give yourself the gift of gratitude morning and night and allow appreciation to seep into your day and into your dreams. Create a habitually grateful mind by keeping a gratitude journal or, if you have a writing practice, adding gratitude to the mix. Take as little as a minute or two at the beginning and end of each day to write down what you are grateful for. Studies at The Greater Good Science Center in Berkeley (n.d.) indicate that just three things written down at the start and end of the day can be sufficient to create positive impact via multiple measures.

As you do this practice at the beginning of the day, you might include gratitude for what is to happen during the day ahead. This is a great way to explore your creative power. If you know there is a beautiful event happening, such as lunch with a friend, imagine it and feel grateful. If there is a challenge ahead, imagine conquering it and feel grateful. At the end of the day, we can reflect on gratitude for what we enjoyed or nourished us, and what challenged us to learn or become more skillful.

To make the most of your neuroplasticity, do this every day for twenty-eight days. This is beyond the twenty-one-day minimum understood to be necessary to create a habit; let's stack the odds in favor of successfully habituating. We can utilize what we know about the science of forming habits to create a grateful autopilot within your brain. Just as gambling, brushing your teeth, biting your nails, or getting up at a certain time can become automated, so too can a grateful mind. Just as driving is largely done by unconscious processes—via the basal ganglia's functioning—by freeing up the prefrontal cortex for other activities and decision making, we can input gratitude consistently such that it happens without will or effort.

In *The Power of Habit*, Charles Duhigg (2012) collates the various insights in this area and highlights a three-step process of habit formation. We can consciously use this to make any desirable activity or pattern of thinking or feeling habitual.

1. The cue or trigger: what sets the brain up to perform the process

2. The routine: the actual activity

3. The reward: the way the brain knows to do this
    again

The cue or trigger in our twenty-eight days could be getting out of bed and getting into bed. To be precise, you might make it when your feet touch the floor on getting up and then your head hitting the pillow when you go to bed. After each cue, you practice giving attention to at least three things about which you feel appreciation. The reward is the good feeling—the activation of dopamine, serotonin, and other positive-feeling neurotransmitters that you want more of. In repeating this process for twenty-eight days, you will significantly enhance your experience of this time frame and increase the likelihood of the next week or few being similarly optimized.

Before you embark on this experiment, reflect on the previous week and month. How happy have you been? What has the quality of your interactions with others been like? Then repeat this at the end of the experiment, compare the two, and see what you discover. Through this before and after, you will likely gain deeper insight into how your choices, focus, and intention affect your life experience. Begin rejoicing in the creative, positive view and feeling of empowerment that gratitude brings!

Such a practice, however imperfect, can be helpfully viewed as a deposit in your bank of well-being. Unlike your bank account, however, when you withdraw from this account, you are simultaneously depositing, and the neuroplastic process ensures the interest will compound and compound!

The truly great news is that each moment, each day, you have the opportunity to start again. Inevitably the momentum of previous habituating and conditioning, from your life and your ancestors' lifespans, will be at play in your consciousness. The learning of positivity and gratitude is indeed a practice and one in which you are helpfully faced with gentleness and self-forgiveness. As you stutter and stumble, you might see old patterns arise from nowhere amid a well-practiced positivity, forget a practice period, or fail to complete it altogether.

Remember in these times:

1. Your every "deposit" has been recorded within your neurology.

2. Every day you get to start again. This moment gifts the opportunity to start all over again, with what you have learned through failure, fueling success. You really cannot get this wrong because all getting it "wrong" is part of getting it "right"!

Through this constant new beginning, with every effort being recorded, you may see a basic kindness, inbuilt fairness, and fundamental positivity in how this whole human experience is set up.

Thank you.

Chapter 2

Being Fully Alive

In the office building where I worked in charity fundraising as a young man, I recall an advertisement for an energy workshop marketed as a means of improving results by 100 percent. On this flimsy evidence, I convinced my manager to invest in this training for me rather than an Excel training. During the workshop, as I grappled with alien concepts and exercises, I was told that I was "too in my head." I was so in my head that I didn't know what that meant; on hearing a thought, I thought about it. Simple as that. I had lived for twenty or so years without hearing this feedback. I now understand that our consciousness is collectively trained to "think it through," to function primarily—even solely—through thought. This is considered not only normal but preferable.

We have high regard for René Descartes's famous line *Je pense, donc je suis*: "I think, therefore I am." This notion, that the ability to think proves we exist, demonstrates a cultural bias toward the mental. I couldn't even begin to get past this until I was encouraged to inquire, "What is aware of thinking?" Clearly, we are more than our thoughts.

This really hit home a few years later, when on a Zen meditation retreat, we did an exercise in which we were invited to speak with our awareness placed first on thinking and then on "clear, deep heart-mind." I had been practicing a lot of qigong and yoga, so I had developed an awareness of my body that I didn't have previously. There was a profound difference between speaking from my thinking head and speaking from my feeling heart: the tone and cadence were different. It felt worlds apart. And speaking from my heart was so much more enjoyable! I began to practice bringing awareness into my heart while talking with people, and discovered how much more pleasant the experience was for everyone. There was an experience of feeling immediate gratitude for this discovery and for finding myself to be such a whole, vast being.

Affirmation: *"I am a whole, vast being feeling grateful for all gateways to knowing."*

What am I? Why am I here? What is the meaning of life? That you are reading this book suggests you have likely found it necessary to ask such questions, and to find your own answers. Let's continue the inquiry.

It is easy to see you are not your body, but rather, have a body. When your body changes, such as a radically different haircut or even the loss of limbs, you are still you. It is subtler yet easy enough to see that in a similar way, you are not your thoughts, feelings, or sensations. If thoughts, feelings, or sensations change, or even if they totally cease, you are still here. Thoughts, feelings, and sensations are things that "what you are" experiences. Pause for a moment and notice any thoughts, feelings, or sensations. See if you can recognize that they are the objects of awareness, what is being seen or perceived. Thus, can you recognize that you must be something other than objects of awareness? You are the subjective perceiving or witnessing. How does it feel to know yourself as a seeing, as awareness, as a process rather than a fixed event or identity, more verb than noun?

This inquiry can sometimes be a little uncomfortable, but I encourage you to stay curious, much as a child would be with a new experience. Keep asking, "What is this? What am I?"

Each time you pause and notice, asking this sort of inquiry question, you may notice a spaciousness, a vastness even. You can sense the simple experience of being, within which thoughts, sensations, feelings, and identities arise. Perhaps this spaciousness, this witnessing, is a truer, more fundamental identity than the thought of "I."

Recognize that you are an imperfect human, learning and growing through failure and success like everyone else, an evolving self, *becoming*. Can you also recognize that you are at once whole, complete, and perfect *being* in this moment?

Reflect on the extraordinary gift of our times, this information age. We have access to so many wonderful and effective ways to know, inquire, discover, and understand. You likely have a large portion of the totality of human knowledge in your pocket—or perhaps in your hand, if you're using a phone or tablet to read this book! Feel appreciation for the many ways you can, do, and will know.

What if you were to combine this awareness of *becoming* and learning, and this *being* or this identity as what you are? "I am a whole vast being feeling grateful for all gateways to knowing."

I invite you to try it on, like a costume. Say this to yourself or out loud. How does it feel? What other thoughts arise? How does it feel when you affirm this? Let your experience be as it is. If resistance or an inability to feel arises, simply notice that and recognize it as part of your whole vast being learning to consciously choose to feel better and know itself more deeply.

Try repeating it several times, again noticing how it feels and how it impacts your experience.

How might your life experience be altered if you brought this idea of who you are to every challenge, to each emotion, to each moment? How might your life change if this belief underpinned it?

Take a moment to feel appreciation for the inquiry and journey you have just undertaken. Feel grateful for the learning and you, the learner. You may like to set the intention to remember this perspective at a future time when it will be most helpful; you can feel now how it will be to recall this affirmation in that future moment and think back to this chapter.

Meditation: Gratitude as Feeling and Sensation

Gratitude is more powerful when we expand our awareness beyond thinking, with our whole body, awareness, emotions, and sense perceptions. Thinking can lead us to a deeper felt sense of gratefulness and of aliveness. This exercise will help you experience both. You can access an audio version of it at http://www.newharbinger.com/42020.

I invite you to pause for a moment and follow this guided exploration with a gentle curiosity. Be willing to discover something new. There are no right or wrong answers. Ensure you are in a quiet, comfortable place where you will not be disturbed for about five to fifteen minutes.

Close your eyes and take a few long, deep breaths.

Become aware of the breath and sensations in the body.

How is it known that you are alive?

How is it known that you *are?* If thought replies, "Because I am thinking," ask, "How is it known that there is thinking?"

Is there a subtler sense than breathing, feeling, thinking? Is it possible to locate aliveness?

Perhaps aliveness is all these things—breathing, feeling, thinking—together.

Or might it be in between these components of experience?

Or could it be surrounding these components of experience?

Can you locate a sense of the body as a whole?

Can you simply be aware of a single finger, say your left little finger or left little toe?

Is it possible to feel how it is to be a cell in that finger or toe?

Do you notice degrees of aliveness?

Simply sit and continue to explore and notice the feeling of aliveness in your body.

Feel appreciation for all of these aspects of your experience. Can you feel appreciation simply for the fact and experience of being alive right now?

Where does this gratitude show up most noticeably? Where in the body do you feel gratitude?

Reflecting on this exercise, consider how easy or difficult it was to explore the various questions. What came naturally, and what seemed to require more practice? Was there a more developed awareness of aspects of experience at the exercise's completion compared with when you began?

Remember you can come back to this section of pointers and questions any time. You may wish to highlight those that you enjoyed the most, or found most difficult, to come back to and try again.

As you continue to familiarize yourself with this body awareness, with the sense of aliveness permeating every cell, you can drop into this felt awareness for a moment or two when going about your day. Even if you had a tense or tedious meeting at work or your children are especially active and demanding of your care and attention, take a moment to breathe deeply and enjoy the feeling of being alive and of feeling grateful for this being. Reflect that this "resource" is with you in whatever experience you encounter in life.

The Magnitude of the Heart

Neuroscience offers an evidence-based explanation for why we can experience knowing all over our body. It offers a scientific explanation for the common notions of "following your heart" or "feeling it in your gut."

We have neurological functioning in our heart, as well as in our gut, and of course in our brain. Our physiology of intelligence is dispersed throughout the body.

The results of measuring the electromagnetic field of different parts of the body are intriguing. First, our heart-brain is sixty times more powerful, electromagnetically, than the head-brain. The magnetic component is five thousand times more powerful! In addition, more energy and information flow up the vagus nerve, from the heart to the brain, than vice versa (Childre and Martin 2000). All of this leads me to question the idea that our head-brain and thinking are the most powerful or effective ways of perceiving or guiding decision making: Is this circumstantial evidence suggesting not only that we are biased and missing out on whole human intelligence but that we may be biased toward a weaker component of it?

Take a moment to feel your head and to feel your heart or gut. How do they differ? Can you detect different types of awareness in each? If there were shapes or colors representing head, heart, and gut, what would they be?

The realization that our heart's knowing might be underutilized can prompt us to think about feeling more. We can logically deduce that there is more to intelligence than logical deduction. We can explore the heart's knowing or intuitive sense. Just as we can cultivate a higher cognitive functioning through use and engagement, can we do the same with our heart's intelligence?

Think of a time that you "just knew" something or "felt it in your gut." You may recall being successfully guided by these deep impulses. You may also recall ignoring them and going with the calculations of thought. What does reflecting on these experiences tell you?

There do appear to be some advantages to developing a greater utility of the intelligence of our gut and heart, the whole of our body's intelligence. While thought is so good at considering the pros and the cons, it can get lost in a time-consuming process of comparing possible paths. Knowing or intuition, on the other hand, typically arrives at an answer instantaneously. Perhaps you can recall meeting someone and immediately knowing—through either feeling good or feeling bad—that they were to be embraced or avoided. In my experience, as we continue to cultivate this heart awareness and intuitive capacity, we can find similar clarity on all manner of other decisions. Choosing and thus life in general can become easier, more reliable, and more effortless by following the heart. Perhaps like me, you can feel a gratitude for your whole intelligence—a grateful, intuitive heart, integrated with sound reasoning, logic, and gut feeling!

There was a time when IQ was *thought* to be a sufficient indicator of intelligence and the cognitive functioning it measures was thought to be essentially what intelligence is. In 1983, Harvard scientist Howard Gardner's (2006) work on multiple intelligences opened us to the view that we have at least seven recognizable, measurable, and equally valuable intelligences.

Dan Goleman's 1995 book, *Emotional Intelligence*, built on the work of researchers Peter Salavoy and John Mayer, focused on the intrapersonal and interpersonal types of intelligence. The book concluded that EQ—the ability to recognize,

understand, and manage our emotions—was just as important an indicator of success as IQ (Goleman 2005). Once
again, by reason and thought, we are led to give more attention to intuition and feeling. Developing our capacity to feel
gratitude does just that. Let's continue with an exercise to
shift awareness into where we feel emotions and develop our
whole human intelligence further.

Exercise: Movement to Expand Awareness

One of my favorite regular physical postures is a perfect
embodiment of gratitude and an easy and effective way to
bring more consciousness into the heart. Any insight or learning is only as real as the extent we act on or from it. We can
have all the lofty spiritual concepts, but embodiment is where
the value is. In this posture, we can embody gratitude in a
very real and immediate way plus enjoy a taste of what we will
explore further in chapter 4—our sensational body.

I enjoy beginning my day with this, incorporating it with
the grateful recognition practice as the first thing I do when
getting out of bed, when my feet touch the floor. It is a helpful
response to whatever feeling I wake up with!

Standing up straight, make sure you have at least an
arm's length of room to move in each direction—
ideally a meter in front and behind and to the left and
right.

Take a deep breath or two, enjoying the experience of your lungs filling with and emptying of air, receiving the gift of oxygen.

Bring your hands together atop your chest, left hand beneath right for men, vice versa for women. This reflects qigong teaching about the typical constitution of the energy body in the male and female, particularly how it relates to the flow of masculine and feminine energy or consciousness in each side of both the male and female body.

Taking a step back with your left leg, simultaneously open your arms wide as far behind your shoulders as is comfortable, opening the chest. As you do so, bring attention to the stretch, tension, or anything else you feel in the center of your chest. Take a deep breath into the center of your chest.

Feel how it is to consciously receive the breath into your open heart.

Bring your arms back into the center, palms together in a prayer pose, if you wish. While the focus is on feeling the body and feeling the heart, you may wish to use thought to express thanks. You might say, out loud or silently, "Thank you for this breath, this body, this beautiful day."

Repeat by taking a step back with the right foot and going through the same process as you did with the left.

Once you are comfortable with the how, after a few repetitions, repeat as mindfully as possible. Slow it down and savor each touch point, each stretch, even each wobble or hesitation.

Reflect on how it is to consciously receive breath. How does it feel to simply enjoy breathing, and the feelings of your body, of your heart? Notice if there is any resistance. This might include ideas that you should be doing something or looking after someone else rather than enjoying your own experience. Consider that giving yourself a good feeling and enjoying breathing and your body is a valid activity in its own right. See that your feeling good benefits everyone you interact with.

You can adapt this simple posture to your needs and ability, doing as many repetitions as you wish, adjusting the affirmation, and so on.

Imagine how your life might be enhanced by beginning each day enjoying the body and breath and feeling grateful for them. Remember, this is for the sake of both your well-being and peace of mind and for those of people you spend time with. Ponder how a deepened awareness and appreciation of your body and your breathing could affect your quality of life overall.

Becoming a Turbocharged Being

The world can certainly seem like it would benefit from *more* reason, logic, and rational, critical thinking, yet I suggest the mental dimension of perception is most effective, indeed turbocharged, when allied with intuitive knowing. As we have seen, the human physiology is designed to have different intelligences concentrated in different areas around the body. Just as the body moves best and most naturally when every cell is functioning in fully activated, optimum condition, we can imagine the same to be true of our whole being expressing its fullest potential through a whole human intelligence. And gratitude is one means by which we can activate, engage, and express this intelligence.

I see gratitude, much like water, sleep, and meditation, as a very effective way of allowing the experience of aliveness, of vibrancy, and of well-being to be ongoing. Regular high-quality intake of all four can be a simple yet powerful way of turbocharging our whole being. These are the most impactful "dials" which can be adjusted to radically transform the very frequency of our lives. It is encouraging that such basics of human flourishing as meditation, emotional resilience, and similar programs are increasingly offered in schools around the world. Much of what I have had to learn and unlearn, and the suffering that prompted this, is being avoided for a new generation of human beings.

Imagine a world in which we taught all our children these perspectives and capacities, giving them the time and guidance to grow into their fullest being, happiness, and fulfillment. Imagine a world of leaders, politicians, CEOs, scientists, and parents who have learned to fully activate this whole human intelligence. Recognize that your inner work in this regard is a direct contribution to a more wholly intelligent world. Observe how your transformation affects your family and their family. Imagine this rippling into the community and society as a whole. Notice how gratitude for all of life, for your role in the evolving human story, supports feeling fully alive, connected, and in well-being.

Thank you.

Chapter 3

A Vehicle for Present-Moment Awareness

It was through a scan consequent to a grand mal seizure that I became aware I had a brain tumor. In this experience, an altered state of consciousness—or "aura" as doctors refer it—was accompanied by a particular tingling in my left hand before I lost consciousness and my body fell to the floor in a spasming epileptic fit or convulsion. Clearly such an experience is undesirable, extremely impractical, and potentially dangerous. Though it is more unpleasant for those witnessing, being unconscious beyond the precursor experience, I resolved to ensure these fits did not continue. The medical advice was to take antiseizure medication. However, in researching the various medicines offered, I discovered they often did not work in preventing seizures, might *cause* seizures or even death, had other serious side effects, and were a nightmare to withdraw from. Thus I ruled out these medicines. Despite being advised I would need to be on them for the rest of my life to avoid seizures, I have not taken a single pharmaceutical pill in well over five years, nor have I had a single grand mal seizure. Intriguingly, gratitude, present-moment awareness, and breath have been my tools to create a healthy and stable brain, even after a significant chunk of it had been removed.

I began by being grateful for this problem of having seizures—grateful because, like the brain tumor diagnosis itself, I felt confident it would provide tremendous opportunity for personal growth and learning. In an immediate and practical application of this, I practiced being grateful for the precursor experience of the aura and tingling in the left hand rather than resisting or pushing it away. This enabled me to bring present-moment awareness to the experience. I noticed that when I became aware of the aura and tingling, a strong fear would arise in my body and thoughts. I stayed present to this and asked, "What am I afraid of?" "Death and/or seizure" was the response. Seeing that the unwillingness to have either experience created a tremendous tension, I chose to surrender to both experiences—I became willing to have a seizure now and to die now. Quite simply, it was clear that in each case, if it was going to happen, it was going to happen, and resistance simply created stress and tension. Stress and tension would, if anything, create a more seizure-prone body. This gratitude for precursor phenomena and possible outcomes led to a willingness and release of my tension and preoccupation with avoidance. This allowed there to simply be awareness of what was happening. From this awareness, I naturally began to utilize breathing practices I had learned previously.

A paradoxical mix of total surrender and willful breathing became my medicine. By breathing deeply and intently into the center of my chest, I learned how to bring my body back into balance. In this way, I managed to avoid seizures and harmful medicines. I am of course only one person. However,

I have since learned of others who have taught themselves a very similar technique for managing seizures. Ultimately, whether you believe this or not, the techniques I utilize can be applied by anyone to access a deep sense of empowerment and confidence. This illustrates the power of gratitude and its relationship with present-moment awareness.

Gratitude can only be felt now, and it is in this moment that we discover the full power of our awareness. We may come to directly experience the delightful paradox that in being with things just as they are, they change. To bring full conscious awareness to emotion and bodily dysfunction is discovered to be "doing something," though it involves doing nothing! The capacity to simply be aware, to observe, is a causative aspect of reality unfolding. Learning to rest here supports the end of suffering, and the discovery of peace and even joy, in any moment. Cultivating gratitude and present-moment awareness are complementary paths to peace and joy.

Affirmation: "I am here, now, aware."

We are gaining greater familiarity with the feeling of gratefulness and how to evoke it in our body and in different circumstances. We may begin to notice that like many qualities we seek—happiness, calm, awakening, to name a few—it can only be found *now*. Similarly, to evoke gratitude, to open our arms, literally or metaphorically, and proclaim, "Yes! Thank you!" is to bring us more fully into present-moment awareness.

While egomind—the self-referencing thought system that makes everything about "me" or "I"—exists in time, thinking of a time in the past when I was happier or of a time in the future when I will be happier, present-moment awareness is always here now and knows no lack. Present-moment awareness is already grateful. In this way, I use the Zen terms of the "pathless path" and "gateless gate" to point to the paradox of seeking. We seek to find and use meditation, gratitude, or whatever approach suits our uniqueness, yet the very tendency to seek can obscure enjoying the presence we already are. After journeying a particular path or moving through a particular barrier, we can observe from the other side that it only existed as a concept in the mind, real only in our imagining— hence, the pathless path and the gateless gate. So, let us honor the value and function of seeking, including the impulse that brought you to this book. Keep in mind that finding is our deepest desire, and finding happens now and has in a very true sense already happened. Much of awakening is simply remembering rather than discovering anything new.

I love how a simple thank-you said or simply felt to life, to God, to the universe, to awareness—take your pick—can restore clarity.

This may all seem a little hard for the thinking mind to grasp, which it inevitably is; just as we cannot bite our own teeth, the mind cannot contain or understand itself. While gratitude uses the thinking mind, it takes us beyond it to our feeling body.

Happily, there are three ever-present steps, or keys, that we can practice bringing awareness to in order to bring us back to the peace, happiness, and contentment of the present moment.

Meditation: Being, Breath, and Awareness

In every moment, no matter the contents of our relative experience or whether we are consciously creating meaning or perceiving habitually and perhaps painfully, there are three things to be grateful for.

Whether being diagnosed with brain cancer or discovering we are all clear, whether taking our first or last breath, feeling the greatest expansive bliss or the most uncomfortably contracted despair, there are three elements to explore bringing attention to.

Being: The embodied centeredness of experience. I am.

Breath: The movement in and out, happening all by itself, that can be played with and directed. I am breathing. I am breath. I am being breathed.

Awareness: The background of all experience. That which right now is aware of these words, aware of the reading, the thoughts, the page, the text. The noticing. I am aware. I am awareness.

You will notice that each is in many ways interchange-able—three aspects of the one experience. It is helpful to con-ceive of three for we all have different tendencies and one may work as an access point for us better than the rest.

Using the exercises in this book, you may master "drop-ping into being," "enjoying breath," or simply "being aware," and you have the capacity to end suffering whenever it might arise. You have three pathless paths back to this precious moment, where you encounter peace and joy. Each of these meditations is so simple as to make instruction superfluous and potentially unnecessarily complicating. In each case, you can practice formally—sit in correct posture and so on—or simply experiment and enjoy next time you are washing dishes or doing some other task.

To drop into being is simply to notice the space between, before, beyond, and surrounding thoughts, and rest there a while. Can you notice being now, not as a thought but as an experience, as the experiencing? Of course you can! Simply notice and ignore any thoughts to the contrary.

Similarly, become fully aware of breathing. Recognize it is giving you, the trees, and every being life, and that is a gift. Breathing breathes, generally requiring no participation from you. Enjoy a few breaths.

Finally, become aware of being aware. Notice awareness. Notice the miracle and mystery of being aware of being aware!

Being, breath, and awareness: three pointers, abundant aspects of every moment of your life, and each a reason to be grateful. Play with these pointers. Go sit for hours focusing on nothing else, or recall each naturally as you go about your day.

Like anything, it just takes a little, or a lot, of practice. Paradoxically, peace is at once a total letting go of the effort of practice such that each moment is a meditation. We may still choose to utilize particular activities we enjoy—personally I "in joy" yoga, qigong, and sitting meditation—yet the quality of our moment-to-moment experience is such that it is not accurate to divide life into practicing and not practicing. Our whole life becomes one ongoing practice. May the entirety of our life, pleasant and unpleasant, become fully present and aware, ever curious, ever grateful. As mentioned in the introduction, the practicing of gratitude creates a more grateful brain over time, such that we might need to practice less formally. Let's look at the evidence for the positive effects of present-moment awareness.

Doing Nothing Does Something: Meditation Works

Meditation in its multitude of forms has been a practice for well-being, transformation, and spiritual awakening for millennia. Of course, it's not really doing nothing, but a highly engaged doing that with practice becomes a nondoing. Much effort is typically required to develop concentration of attention, and after a while this becomes effortless. Over the last several decades, meditation has been an increasingly studied phenomenon, and we have learned much about its effects upon the mind, brain, mental health, and physical health. I personally credit meditation with huge benefits in my life. I often think it is much like water or indeed gratitude—something that is necessary to imbibe regularly for optimum functioning and well-being. However, I have also been aware that it is hard to really know the primary cause of transformation. This is because I have often adopted several changes at once, so it is hard to pinpoint which is most impactful. From age twenty-one, I began exercising regularly, practicing martial arts and yoga, going to counseling, following a vegetarian diet, and living in another country (anyone who has visited Australia or New Zealand will likely be open to the possibility that this alone may have positive effects on well-being!). In addition, I am of course naturally going to be biased and lack objectivity. Decades of applying the scientific method to the study of meditation must surely give us a clear picture of how it works and the benefits it has, right?

Yes and no. In *Altered Traits: Science Reveals How Meditation Changes Your Mind, Brain and Body*, Daniel Goleman and Richard J. Davidson (2017) reveal much about what we don't know due to methodological limitations and the inherent challenge of studying objectively subjective experience. However, it is clear the field is advancing as it grapples with such challenges and as technology improves. There is certainly evidence we have reason to be grateful for meditation's beneficial effects on both physical and mental health.

The authors summarize the physical benefits thus:

> None of the many forms of meditation studied here was originally designed to treat illness, at least as we recognize it in the West. Yet today the scientific literature is replete with studies assessing whether these ancient practices might be useful for treating just such illnesses. MBSR [mindfulness-based stress reduction] and similar methods can reduce the emotional component of suffering from disease, but not cure those maladies. Yet mindfulness training—even as short as three days—produces a short-term decrease in pro-inflammatory cytokines, the molecules responsible for inflammation. And the more you practice, the lower the level becomes of these pro-inflammatory cytokines. This seems to become a trait effect with extensive practice, with imaging studies finding in meditators at rest lower levels of pro-inflammatory cytokines, along with an increased connectivity between regulatory circuitry and sectors of the brain's self system, particularly the posterior cingulate cortex. Among experienced meditation practitioners, a daylong period of intensive mindfulness practice down-regulates genes involved in inflammation. The enzyme telomerase, which slows

cellular aging, increases after three months of intensive practice of mindfulness and loving-kindness. Finally, long-term meditation may lead to beneficial structural changes in the brain, though current evidence is inconclusive about whether such effects emerge with relatively short-term practice like MBSR, or only become apparent with longer-term practice. All in all, the hints of neural rewiring that undergird altered traits seem scientifically credible, though we await further studies for specifics. (Goleman and Davidson 2017, 206)

As for the benefits for mental health through meditation, there is "promise in the treatment of some, particularly depression and anxiety disorders. In a meta-analysis of forty-seven studies on the application of meditation methods to treat patients with mental health problems, the findings show that meditation can lead to decreases in depression (particularly severe depression), anxiety, and pain—about as much as medications but with no side effects. Meditation also can, to a lesser degree, reduce the toll of psychological stress. Loving-kindness meditation may be particularly helpful to patients suffering from trauma, especially those with PTSD" (Goleman and Davidson 2017, 225).

Exercise: Living a Radically Grateful Life

It is beyond this book to provide a detailed outline of the vastly complex varieties, styles, and functions of meditation. Fortunately, there are a huge number of resources available these days—such as meditation classes from Zen, transcendental meditation, Sri Chinmoy, Brahma Kumaris, or mindfulness via a local group, course, or app—to support your meditation practice. Here, I will highlight two stages of meditation which generally form the first two steps of many wisdom traditions—concentration and open awareness—in the form of two practices. In each instance, find a comfortable sitting position, with your back straight, and set a timer for your selected duration. Follow each meditation with the mini-practice Grateful Awareness.

Concentration Meditation

Whether a mantra, candle flame, bodily sensation, or breath, the same principle underlies all these apparently different practices: training our concentration and developing our ability to sustain our focus upon a single point. For this meditation, pick one thing to focus on and stick with it. If you are just beginning, it might be most helpful to choose a more tangible item for concentration, such as a mantra (which could be a spiritual poem or prayer repeated silently) or bodily sensation, rather than something subtler, such as breath. In developing the capacity to concentrate through more tangible objects, you will find it easier to follow the breath later.

Ideally when beginning meditation, we practice this method for an hour in the morning and an hour in the evening for a year or two for the best results. Of course, this is often not going to be practical. Equally, twenty minutes morning and night for eight weeks will create measurable change.

Open Awareness Meditation

Once our practice of concentration has developed, we can, from this laser focus, allow awareness to disperse. We can now practice "just sitting," simply being aware. Thoughts, sensations, concentration, no concentration, feelings, sensory data, all can arise without effort or strain.

If you do not currently have a daily meditation practice, I encourage you to begin a concentration practice. It might involve sitting or walking, as described above, or a form of movement such as dance, yoga, or qigong, which can be meditative disciplines through which concentration is developed. This timeless activity goes hand in hand with gratitude. To see this clearly, consider the below mini-exercise.

Grateful Awareness

Take a moment to think of aspects of your life that you appreciate. Notice this involves being more aware. Now take a few moments to simply be aware. Notice that in this pausing, in simply being, a gratitude naturally and effortlessly arises for all phenomena, for being itself. This interchangeability of gratitude and awareness will become more evident as we practice each more and more.

This awesome circle—the opposite of a vicious circle—is a natural consequence of curiosity into your own experience and the willingness to cultivate gratitude, both cause and consequence of present-moment awareness.

The Mystery of Consciousness

How can doing nothing appear to do something? This question is similar to many of the questions surrounding what the philosopher and cognitive scientist David Chalmers in 1995 labeled the "hard problem of consciousness" (Chalmers 1999). This was an acceptance of the mystery of our experience of being conscious and how little is known about the relationship between physical brain processes and the related phenomena of experience. The central question of the hard problem is often framed as: How does immaterial consciousness come from a material brain? Though this is the commonly accepted hard problem, you could just as easily remove an unstated assumption (that matter is primary or causative) and reverse the phrase to ask: How does the material brain come from immaterial consciousness? It is my reasoned view and subjective knowing that consciousness is in fact primary.

However, whether you favor putting the egg or the chicken first, the relationship between the two is at the core of present-moment awareness and its interacting with any event, whether that is experiencing a grand mal seizure, enjoying a chocolate brownie, or grappling with big concepts while reading a book.

The primacy of consciousness can be reasoned to be supported by one of the most repeated and perplexing experiments of science: the double-slit experiment, which shows that the act of observing something, like a particle, dramatically affects its behavior and function. The act of observing appears to determine what is being observed. It might be fair to say that this experiment, along with many others at the beginning of the twentieth century, turned physics on its head in a way so complete and paradoxically confusing that we have yet to recover.

Prior to the development of quantum mechanics through the work of Max Planck, Niels Bohr, Wolfgang Pauli, Erwin Schrödinger, Sir James Jeans, and Arthur Eddington from 1905 to 1920, we were comfortable with our understanding of the world gained via the highly effective Newtonian or classical mechanics. Here, cause and effect is the key principle in a linear unfolding of an objective, predictable reality. It was in many ways inconvenient to discover that the quantum view is simultaneously true, in which synchronicity is the key principle in a nonlinear unfolding of a subjective, unpredictable reality—a reality where, as the double-slit experiment shows, consciousness is a causative agent in the physical taking form.

Entanglement further loosens the solidity of ideas such as inner and outer, subjective and objective, even time and space. Though the exact implications of the data are still very much debated (there are perhaps eleven distinct schools of thought!), I am inclined toward the von Neumann–Wigner interpretation (named after the Hungarian American mathematician, physicist, and polymath John von Neumann and Eugene Wigner, a US Nobel laureate physicist), in which the observing consciousness is posited as the collapser of the wave function (von Neumann 1932; Wigner 1967). In layman's terms, *observation informs matter*. With this view in mind, the value, power, and importance of your creating the universe *gratefully* is supported. If consciousness is informing the physical universe, and the nature or intention of that consciousness is causative, we would be wise to ensure that the nature and intention of our perceptions, thoughts, and beliefs is aligned with what we desire to experience. This further supports the idea presented in chapter 1 that heaven and hell are states of consciousness that are only a hair's breadth apart. Adding this quantum view into the mix, we might regard them as coexisting probabilities that we may activate, create, and experience through our intention and attention. Though prior to quantum mechanics, William Blake (1906) evokes this idea succinctly in stating, simply: "Gratitude is heaven itself."

This guides us to gratitude's interrelation with present-moment awareness and the power of both. The brief summary of the infinitely complex topic of quantum mechanics gives your mind the lens through which it may comprehend what ultimately is best directly experienced. Here words are truly inadequate, but let us say "oneness," or "truth," or, as I prefer, "*this*": This that is aware, here, everywhere, now, and always. *This* that is most truly you and all you will ever experience (including the experience of you!). *This* that is grateful beyond words for it all, for the universe it has created in order to know and experience itself.

How truly wonderful to play with *this*, being, being grateful, grateful being. And, perhaps, to know it as an interplay of all that is, experiencing and loving itself as it infinitely and eternally unfolds. We are the universe expanding.

In the next chapter, we will explore gratitude for the mysterious miracle by which this happens as your sensational human body.

Thank you.

PART 2

Becoming Grateful for Your Entire Life

Chapter 4

Your Sensational Body

The human body is ultimately a mystery, a miracle, if you will. We know that it comprises somewhere between 15 and 70 trillion cells depending on how you measure—a fairly wide range! We know with considerably more precision that there are eleven important organ systems, most prominently the circulatory, respiratory, digestive, excretory, nervous, immune, and endocrine systems. We also know a great deal about how each of these discrete systems functions and interacts. We know enough to evoke a deep sense of awe, wonder, and appreciation for our body. Take a moment right now to feel appreciation for your trillions of cells, each of the eleven systems, and the whole functioning that is happening every moment without your effort or will.

What we really don't know is the bigger how or why. How is it that I am being breathed? How does the cell know to be cellular? What is the nature of the immense intelligence that, every second, coordinates this infinitely complex system?

With such questions, we stray into the philosophical, religious, or spiritual, and as much as our scientific mind will assert what we do know, it must accept that there is far more that we don't know—including how or why it is that in contemplating the mystery and magnitude, we experience awe, wonder, or consciousness of this at all. It is in this sense that it is inexplicable. The term "miracle," as religiously loaded as it is, feels valid and accurate.

Mysterious, too, is how the awesome intelligence of the body appears to falter, such as in the forming of a brain tumor. Beyond the philosophical ponderings, answering how this happens has a very practical application. Of course, I asked this very question: What caused my brain to develop a tumor? I put the question many times to several neurologists, oncologists, neurosurgeons, neuro-oncologists, energy healers, naturopaths, and shamans. The most common answer, particularly from the conventional medical group—and I am grateful for the humility and candor of my team of professionals—was, "We don't know." The shaman, perhaps unexpectedly, said it was from hitting my head as a child. I had expected a verdict of entities, past lives, demons, or some similarly glamorous deep psychospiritual insight. Instead, it was the humdrum of hitting my head! The two concussions experienced one week after the other playing rugby as a teenager were reasonable causes.

I also asked myself, my own body, how the tumor formed. I even asked the tumor directly and listened to my intuition and felt sense. The answer that formed is a tapestry of causative threads: from smoking as a teenager to the head trauma while playing rugby to the use of a mobile phone held to my head for several hours at a time. The 2011 Danish Cohort Study (Frei et al. 2011) published in the *British Medical Journal* that the mobile phone companies reference as evidence of no cause for alarm is dismissed by, among others, the Professor Emeritus of Radiation Studies at Bristol University, Denis Henshaw, as being worthless due to an absence of longitudinal and high-use data (Henshaw 2011). Meanwhile, several studies including a 2004 Canadian paper (Momoli et al. 2017) that includes these factors suggests a 40 percent increase in glioma occurrence when high daily use occurs over five-plus years. The World Health Organization (2014) lists the electromagnetic fields produced by mobile phones as a possible carcinogen. I recall experiencing a very hot head on the side I used the phone, getting headaches, and wondering how I might minimize the potential danger. Now, I endeavor to minimize use, avoid contact with the body, and limit exposure to electromagnetic radiation in general, which is a real challenge in this world.

However, when it comes to what caused the brain tumor, it is another causative thread that I am most interested in. While there are limits to directly remedying the likely damage from electromagnetic radiation, this thread has the benefit of prompting a practical response to create health.

I had been studying mind-body medicine, energy healing, spontaneous remissions, and the placebo effect as part of broader research into the nature of consciousness for many years prior to the diagnosis, and thus looking to how my thoughts and emotions played a causative role in the tumor was inevitable. Though the shaman saw only a physical cause,

I was struck by the coincidence of my experience of suicidal depression and the brain tumor's nature and location.

When I was in the grips of depression—on and off from my early teens to early twenties—there was a visual that accompanied the thought, *I can always kill myself.* This visual was a gun to my head, pointed directly to where the tumor was located. The tumor was largely a cyst—if one were to imagine a bullet going into the brain and what it might look like, the MRI of my brain might not be far from it, with the cyst representing the explosive impact. Could it be that this intense self-loathing, deeply felt worthlessness, and wish to die expressed through unconscious visualizing was another thread in the tumor's manifestation?

Now I am aware I might be losing you in this. You might reasonably be thinking, *This guy thinks he visualized his brain tumor!* To be clear, I am suggesting it was simply one causative thread of many. And the science of psychoneuroimmunology and studies of visualization's power provide support for this line of thinking. The validity of visualizing tumor reduction as a complementary approach is accepted, even within mainstream medicine. If consistent imagining when associated with a strong emotion can be a contributory cure of cancer, it stands to reason it could also be a cause. And in identifying this cause, might I find the cure?

Through much in-depth personal inquiry and healing work, it became clear to me that my desire to die and feeling disconnected from love were causative factors. Thus, I had a remedy: a desire to live and learn to receive love in ever more fully embodied ways. As the title of my first book, *Blessed with a Brain Tumor*, indicates, I began by loving the tumor, a part of me. I have enjoyed and benefited immeasurably from learning to open to receive love from life in all kinds of ways, not only from my father and whole family but from every breath I consciously inhale and each moment I consciously am. Gratitude has been the primary means for creating this.

Indeed, a recent admission to the hospital consequent to an intense altered state of consciousness was treated via breathing in love, a self-taught treatment rather than anything mainstream medicine offered. I have since learned from a distinguished expert on emotional resilience and its cultivation, Linda Graham, MFT, that placing a hand on our heart and taking conscious breaths is something she teaches in her workshops. (You can enjoy this conversation and many others on my podcast, The TruthLover, at https://loveandtruthparty .podbean.com.) In practicing gratitude and bringing awareness into this sensational body, we are bringing the positive effects of this treatment into our everyday experience.

Affirmation: *"I am grateful to be experiencing such a beautiful body."*

Being human is intense; being in a body means pain. The Shakespearian maxim "To be, or not to be?" is a natural question to arise in such conditions. This, too, can be met and acknowledged. Let's look for deeper truths.

I invite you to take a moment to view the body with great appreciation for all it has endured and carried you through. Consider all the toxins it processes every second and the oxygen it is now extracting from that breath and dispersing through itself. Though it may sound silly, take a moment to cuddle yourself, caress yourself. The good news is that your brain does not know the difference between you cuddling yourself and another cuddling you. Give yourself the experience of being held.

Whatever you think about your body's apparent flaws, recognize that overall it is beautiful in its breathing, digesting, sensing. Recognize that your fingerprint, your unique expression, has unique value. More fundamentally, appreciate that it is central to this whole human experience of being, good and bad.

With this in mind, connect with your body and repeat the affirmation: *I am grateful to be experiencing such a beautiful body.* Throw in more cuddling. For a few minutes, repeat the affirmation and cuddle yourself.

How does it feel to love and appreciate your sensational body? What becomes possible within the discovery that you can give yourself the experience of feeling appreciated and loved?

Meditation: Knowing Your Body Is Literally Sensational

It is one thing to think that your body is sensational, another to know. Let's now enjoy a meditation to give this experience. You can download an audio version at http://www.newharbin ger.com/42020.

Find a quiet spot and sit comfortably. Set your timer for fifteen minutes.

Set the intention not to move your body before the time is up.

Begin by taking a few deep breaths to bring awareness into the body.

Bring awareness into the left little toe, across the toes, into the ball of the foot, into the sole of the foot, the heel, the inner and outer ankle, and the Achilles tendon. Methodically bring awareness up through your calf into the shin, knee, thigh, genitalia, hip, left little finger, left palm, thumb, lower arm, elbow, upper arm, armpit. Scan down the abdomen and up the back to the neck and left side of the face, chin, jaw, lips, upper lip, nose, cheeks, eyes, eyebrow, forehead, temple, scalp, crown.

Repeat this process going down the right side and ending in the little toe of the right foot.

This body scan meditation is a beginner's concentration practice. Contemplate these questions:

1. How is it that you are aware of any part of the body?

2. Does the feeling of sensation vary in degree and quality—warm/hot, blocked/open—in different parts of the body?

3. Does this vary in the same parts of the body at different times?

4. What happens when you don't wriggle away but instead sit with sensation the mind has labeled as "painful"?

5. What is the result of discovering directly that what you thought was fixed and unbearable is, in fact, fluid and bearable?

This practice is great for increasing body awareness. Remember, it is in our sensational bodies that we feel grateful. It also gives key insights—such as that everything is impermanent and that this too will pass—and develops emotional resilience. The act of being with the painful sensation in my knee, for example, is much the same as being with the painful feeling of sadness or guilt. Each, when fully faced and felt, flows on easily. In this we can learn to be grateful for all sensation as sensation, rather than dividing sensations into good and bad.

The Placebo Effect, Epigenetics, and Creating Not-So-Spontaneous Remission

There are two key principles to create health from chronic disease that can be very helpful in developing appreciation for our sensational bodies. The placebo effect and epigenetics both demonstrate the remarkable complexity and capacity of the body. My interest is particularly in relation to the beliefs, thoughts, feelings, and emotions we experience.

The placebo effect is a beneficial effect produced by a sugar pill, dummy drug, or treatment that cannot be attributed to the properties of the placebo itself and must therefore be due to the patient's belief in that treatment. Put simply, under the placebo effect, if you believe you are going to experience less pain, your body will produce pain relief. If you believe that you are going to feel happier or more peaceful, your body will create this experience. If you believe you are going to die in six months or live for many more decades, either scenario may become considerably more likely.

Sadly, this remarkable discovery has been treated as an inconvenience of drug companies seeking stats that support a drug's efficacy rather than being applied through empowering communication to patients. As I have already shared, a doctor advised that my attitude was irrelevant in my responding to a cancer diagnosis in such a way as to maximize the likelihood of creating health. Though the subject of psychoneuroimmunology is well established and fairly well accepted within the mainstream, there has overall been a remarkable lack of imagination in applying it. I recall a family member, a doctor who specialized in psychoneuroimmunology for his PhD, stating that psychoneuroimmunology has limited application. Such a belief is itself self-fulfilling. What if every doctor chose to empower patients with the facts: that their attitude, beliefs, and thoughts create sensations and biochemical immune system response in their body? It really should not be the case that only those patients able to access the many self-help books pointing to these scientific facts benefit.

Epigenetics expands our idea of genetics beyond simple determinism to realize that environmental effects such as diet, chemicals, and so forth can cause our genes to express or not. It clarifies that while we are born with a certain genetic blueprint, how or whether our various genes express or not is not predetermined. When we consider that our thoughts and feelings will create a correspondent biochemical experience that can suppress or activate an immune response, it is a logical step to include our thoughts and emotions as epigenetic factors. Bruce Lipton is a leading exponent of this idea in his book *Biology of Belief* (2005). Thus, gratitude practiced consistently can be logically deduced to have a potential effect on your genetic expression through adjusting the physical environment of the body. This potential effect sits alongside all kinds of other positive physical effects. The placebo effect makes it likely that gratitude will be beneficial to your overall well-being regardless of the degree of your mind's influence over your epigenetics.

As mentioned, you may have to access this information yourself rather than rely on doctors being educated about your body's full potential for self-healing. One great such resource is *Radical Remissions* by Kelly Turner (2014). For her PhD, Dr. Turner did something kind of staggering that no one had done before. She decided to study the thousands of cases of spontaneous remission—people who healed from cancer without Western medicine or after Western medicine had failed. That is, she decided to study the most striking examples of the creation of health from disease to find generalities that anyone seeking to create health could apply. I am grateful she did.

Thankfully, the Institute of Noetic Sciences (IONS) had been keeping a database of such examples, and the results of analysis of over fifteen hundred cases established that there were nine key areas that covered what these "outlier" patients attributed to causing their health. Some utilized just one of them; no one covered all nine. Engaging with all nine is now possible with Dr. Turner's work, providing a practical framework. Intriguingly there was one binding element: almost everyone spoke of relying upon their intuition to guide their treatment options.

This is of course the very same gut feeling or heart knowing—the whole human intelligence we began to explore in chapter 2. This provides further reason to develop our awareness of our sensational body, using the exercises in this book, yoga, qigong, bodywork, and more to bring awareness to the ever-changing and communicative sensations of our physical form.

Exercise: Loving Your Whole Body

The human being's full development is dependent upon our being loved and held as babies. We all love being loved and appreciated and yearn to experience this. Even if we think we do not, or are defended or fearful such that we are unable to receive love when offered and deflect compliments, we physiologically and psychologically need to be loved in order to be at our best.

Though our capacity to experience love is hugely affected by the degree to which this was given to us by our caregivers, whatever our experience as children, we can practice giving ourselves love and cuddles as adults. While we cannot control how others think of us or how much they love or embrace us, we are in control of how much we love and embrace ourselves.

For part 1 of this exercise, you will need the largest mirror you can find, ideally full-length. The perfect scenario is a full-length mirror in a quiet room where you know you will not be disturbed. However, it can be adapted with whatever mirror you can access, or by simply looking at or imagining your body. You will need about fifteen minutes.

Standing in front of the mirror, begin to look at your body.

Start to speak, out loud if possible, and *feel* declarations of love for your body and its parts.

Begin with your forehead, temples, eyes, nose, nostrils, lips, tongue, chin, jaw, ears, throat, neck, Adam's apple, and work your way down.

Simple declarations could be "I love you, nose" or "I love you, lips." However, the more detailed they are, the more impactful and deeply felt they will be. I might say, "I love you, beautiful eyes, for helping me to see beauty," or "I love you, kissable lips, for being both so erotic and supporting eating." You get the idea. Have fun with it.

Work your way through the whole body from head to toe.

Ensure you give attention to your unseen parts too— brain, heart, liver, kidney, lungs, and so on.

Feel grateful for every part of your body and all it does.

If working with a small mirror or no mirror at all, simply look at or imagine your lovely body parts.

For part 2, we are going to ground and embody this love and appreciation for our sensational body by hugging ourselves. There are two different self-hugs my community and I enjoy. The first is called the cosmic hug. Standing or sitting, place your hands under your armpits, right hand under the left armpit and left hand under the right, fingers facing behind you and thumbs visible in front of you pointing up. This is the cosmic hug and connects and activates your heart meridian. I am not always good at following instructions, and when this was shared with me I found myself placing hands on top of opposite shoulders. This felt really good too. I call it the very cosmic hug! Try both and see how they feel. Hold each for at least twenty seconds. While it might seem silly to the mind, to the brain this is very similar to being hugged, and I imagine has all sorts of positive effects.

Being Grateful for Being Embodied

Whether we possess 15 trillion or 70 trillion cells or whether we think we have a beautiful or ugly body, we can recognize that there is a truth to every body, including our own: that it is a remarkable, mysterious, even miraculous phenomenon. We undoubtedly take it for granted, perhaps in part due to its excellent capacity for generally functioning very well without our involvement.

With the knowledge that we have gained or been reminded of in this chapter, we can choose to take a moment to celebrate this physical marvel that allows us to have this experience of reading a book right now. Coupled with the insight that the beliefs we hold about our physical reality come into form in a real and measurable way, we may feel inspired to clearly see, develop the belief, and feel in every sensational cell that we have a wonderful body.

Take a moment to reflect on how you have viewed, thought, and felt about your body and consider the advantages of practicing feeling gratitude for all the good aspects and basic functionality of your body.

You may want to once again hug your body and give yourself the experience of being loved—perhaps having checked that the family is not watching or, on the contrary, inviting them to the cuddle party! Looking at your body in the mirror, with this newfound awareness of its miraculous nature, can be another fun experience and means of anchoring or embodying these insights.

This body awareness can create another circle of awesomeness—a self-perpetuating and reinforcing loop of wellbeing. In discovering and creating the feeling of gratitude for and in the body, you are beginning to access a greater potential for intimacy and the experience of being happily embodied, of wanting to be here. We will explore this wisdom of the body in greater depth in chapter 9 when we discuss the purpose of suffering, how it is held in the body, and how radical gratitude can support its cessation.

Thank you.

Chapter 5

Your Unique Self

I came into this world about a month past my due date. I have joked that this was a sign of intelligence: I realized I was onto a good thing, very comfortable, with all my needs met, and I was in no hurry to leave the safety of my mother's womb.

Such a story makes sense within the awareness of some of the curious features we have included in the human being welcoming committee. The fluorescent lighting, the stressful atmosphere, an occasional metal clamp around the head, and being slapped are hardly enticements likely to encourage a baby to be born.

However, there is of course one flaw in this humorous little story: even if there were somehow awareness of these potential greetings, there is no self to be aware of them and thus be put off. We come into this world simply aware, as undifferentiated, undivided awareness and feeling. Looking at a newborn baby tells us this. The child will often appear entirely bewildered, amazed, stunned. Yet we know there is actually no one, no identity, to be amazed. Studies have shown that the idea of "me," the sense of a self, does not appear to form until two to three years old. The curious awareness is told, "This is Mommy, this is Daddy, this is a tree, a dog, a cat, and you are you." In the earliest years, other than through bodily sensation, there is no capacity for a sense of self. As the brain develops, the idea of "me" begins to take hold through thought and language. Scientists developed a revealing experiment that allows the arising sense of me—and thus other—to be tracked as a predictable universal stage of human development.

Faced with a two-sided shape with different colors on each side, the child is asked: What do you see? What does Mommy see? And then the shape is turned so that the child can see there are two sides of different colors. We know that if we are seeing one color, the person on the other side is seeing the other color. However, the younger child still answers the second question with the answer of the first; if I am seeing green, then everyone is seeing green. The arising of a sense of self and other, the beginning of the sense of separation, allows the child to recognize that there is their view and another's view. Only within this expanded awareness, now including a "my" and a "yours," can they correctly answer the question of what the other sees.

We only need pause a moment to consider the value of taking another's perspective, and the problems when people are unable to, to see the clear developmental value of this. Clearly the development of an ego, of a self, is advantageous and evolutionary.

The sense of self continues to develop and form in interrelationship with other phenomena, whether with people—beginning with our primary caregivers, usually Mom and Dad; with feelings, such as hunger, pain, and sadness; or with objects. If there is a you or an it, there is a me. If there is an object, there is a subject. The English language expresses and reinforces this apparent state of affairs very efficiently. Other languages, such as Japanese, are less dualistic. Also, the languages of indigenous peoples often emphasize wholeness rather than separation. I recall watching a recording of a 1970s linguistics conference featuring David Bohm in which a linguist who was also an American Indian shared how his language would say, "Bouncing," rather than "There is a ball bouncing." Within the awareness that our language creates our experience, imagine for a moment a culture that speaks of flow, of movement, of verbs, rather than of subjects and objects. It is likely a challenge, as it requires you to imagine beyond the very structure of thought you are so well accustomed to experiencing life through. If you have always and only been looking through green-colored lenses, it is tricky to imagine what a rose-colored world would look like. Yet, if as Ludwig Wittgenstein states, "the limits of my language are the limits of my world" (1922), and we wish to live without limits, we must take on such perceptual challenges and see beyond our own conditioning.

This elucidates an important point, which is that your self was constructed and formed within this framework of language. Your self was constructed. Me is a construction.

Let's look at ways that a particular self might be formed.

Daddy might see us crying and feel uncomfortable with our emotion. An "I am not safe" self-feeling might form.

Mommy might coo and love us 99 percent of the time, but every moment she is distracted, not present, or apparently withdraws her love, a self might form that says, "I am not loved," or "Love is unreliable." Though I use language to express these senses of self, they may arise without language and exist in the body as felt sensation because thought comes later as the brain develops and tries to make sense of the world and who we are, via ideas, mental constructs of self, and concurrent feeling states in the emotional and physical body.

An emotion arises, and the idea "I am feeling sad" arises. Notice the difference between this and "There is sadness." The idea of me is a nonessential concept added to the experience, which changes the feeling of the experience. Every phenomenon or experience is potentially accompanied by this self-referencing thought. In this way, in every experience, we can see a new self being born—a happy self, a sad self, a despairing self, a joyful self, a confident self, an anxious self, an altruistic self, a selfish self, a content self, a discontent self, a failure self, a successful self. Far more of these "selves" exist in each of us.

We can see that far from there being one continuous fixed self, we have thousands of selves, each formed in response to different experiences, at different times, and held in the body as a particular energetic template—most of which we are not aware of. We come to identify with an idea of who we are that is socially acceptable and hopefully, if we are lucky, functional. I have shared earlier in this book how I came to identify with a dysfunctional self and so consciously created a more functional one. I made up a new me. Of course, this brings the question: Who or what is the "I" that is creating the new me?

We might regard the selves we are not aware of as our inner children. These parts of our psyche were formed in childhood, most often in response to traumatic experience, times when our body-mind appeared to be under threat. The practice of becoming aware of our sensational body, of learning to be with all sensation, comfortable and uncomfortable, of appreciating all of our body, is at once the practice of learning to meet, greet, and love these aspects of ourselves. While we and our parents were once unable to give loving presence, we can now cultivate this loving presence to give to ourselves. We can experience loving and being loved by the consistent practice of being fully present with our experience, which is considerably easier said than done, like all things, and yet doable.

The above story is your story, my story, the basic outline and essence of everyone's story. Yet it fails to include one crucial fact. While our neuroses, fears, dreams, drives, and wishes can be seen as the same as anyone else's, the way they converge in each of us and the shape they form are entirely unique. Just as every snowflake is made of water, and each follows uniform geometric rules yet remains entirely unique, a one-off, so it is with us humans. You are unique, never seen before, and never to be seen again. Allow that to sink in. You are, just like everyone else, a one-off creation. Thus, you play a role no one else can play in this human story. Each one of us plays multiple starring roles in this universal drama, paradoxically as magnificent as we are insignificant, perfect in our imperfection.

Affirmation: *"I am grateful for being as I am, and I love myself as I am."*

How does it feel to let go of all attempts to improve yourself, of all ideas of not being enough, and of anything that includes the idea of your being something other than totally worthy, whole, and complete as you are?

How is it to, just for a moment, accept who you are as you are and that you could not be otherwise? How is it to regard all your neuroses, flaws, imperfections, pains, wounds—everything you have ever rejected or disliked about yourself—and to place them in one perfect bundle of imperfection and embrace it?

As in previous chapters, try repeating the affirmation, utilizing the mental body to generate an adjusted felt and embodied experience: *I am grateful for being as I am, and I love my self as I am.*

How does it feel to repeat this to yourself? When you say it out loud, how does it feel in the body?

Meditation: Loving Your Unique Life

Find a quiet spot, make yourself comfortable, and prepare to go on an inner journey. Put aside at least twenty minutes to walk through your life in imagination and memory. You can access audio for this meditation at http://www.newharbinger.com/42020.

Take a few deep breaths to center and ground your awareness in your body here and now. We are going to relive your life. We are concerned with the broad outline. There is no need to dwell in the pain and trauma of an experience but simply describe the facts as though you were an impartial reporter.

Begin at your birth, imagining as much as you can of the experience, of the medical setup of the time, of your mother, your father. Imagine the city, the hospital, the time in which you were born.

What did you come home to?

Who was your mother at the time; who was your father? Did you have brothers and sisters? How might they have received you?

How was it to be embodied, to have a body, to be hungry, to wet yourself, to vomit, to poo in your pants, to need help doing everything?

Imagine your first birthday. What were you wearing; what did you look like? Who was there? What was the biggest event of the previous year?

Now do the same for your second birthday, the third, and so on.

Using your imagination and curiosity, see what you can recall, what you can sense or intuit, and allow whatever you can perceive to be acceptable.

Continue right up until today having gone through year by year, piecing together your life as best as you can.

On completing the journey, reflect on your life. What hardships have you faced, what difficulties? What accomplishments, what best efforts?

Consider the unique aspects of you too. What makes you, you? How did you show up to life in ways that you can recognize to be somehow "signature" events or responses?

Reflect on the many different ways you have behaved. Can you locate being kind and unkind, smart and stupid, reactive and responsive, proud and ashamed, courageous and fearful?

Ponder as if you were learning about this life story as that of another. How would feel toward this character? How much understanding and compassion would you bring to them? Can you appreciate their efforts, feel grateful for the good they have done?

Complete the meditation by giving this compassion and appreciation to yourself. Take a few moments to cultivate the experience of feeling gently toward your own being.

Divinely You: Identity Beyond Your Self

Curiously, science can find no evidence for this sense of self we all have. There is no "me" center in the brain. The arising of a sense of self, of the doer of actions, the I, appears to be a series of parts of the brain firing together. Known as the default-mode network (DMN), this is naturally active, by default, when daydreaming or at rest but especially when self-referencing thoughts are occurring, when I am thinking about my life narrative or my emotions. It has been speculated that the enlightened state is the activation of the brain in such a way as to transcend the DMN.

In addition to this insight that the neurological basis of the self is dispersed throughout the brain and is more of an activity than actor, Benjamin Libet's famous experiments cast further doubt upon the veracity of self, as we typically perceive of it, or identify as it.

Libet's (1985) experiments involved research participants flexing their wrists or fingers at a moment that they chose while researchers measured the timing of three things:

1. the moment of conscious awareness of an urge to flex the wrist (noted by the participant on a special clock),

2. the moment that electrical activity is recorded in the brain (using an electroencephalogram or EEG of the motor cortex), indicating the brain's initiation of action (known as a "readiness potential"), and

3. the moment that electrical activity is recorded in the muscles of the wrist (electromyogram, EMG), indicating that the voluntary flex was being enacted.

A commonsense idea of how our actions work might cause us to expect that we first have a conscious awareness of an intention or urge to act, and then the brain activates the motor area that sends a signal to the muscles. The surprising thing is that this is not what Libet found.

A predictable finding was that when averaged across participants, the results revealed that activity in the motor area of the brain preceded the electrical activity in the muscle by 550 milliseconds (ms). Our brain activity precedes our muscle activity. Less predictably, the participants' reports of their conscious awareness of the urge to move were only 200 ms prior to the electrical activity recorded in the muscle. Brain activity preceded conscious awareness by about a third of a second! What does this imply?

The brain unconsciously initiates the process of what appears as "voluntary" action. Only following this do we become aware.

The implications of these data have been debated, with many concluding they disprove the idea that we possess free will. We will look at this further in chapter 6. For now, we can conclude that these oft-repeated experiments do appear to support the idea that the sense of self is illusory; that is, it is not as it seems. In Bob Berman and Robert Lanza's excellent *Biocentrism*, we learn of even more startling recent experiments:

> More recent experiments by Libet, announced in 2008, analyzing separate, higher-order brain functions, have allowed his research team to predict up to ten seconds in advance which hand a subject is about to decide to raise. Ten seconds is nearly an eternity when it comes to cognitive decisions, and yet a person's eventual decision could be seen on brain scans that long before the subject was even remotely aware of having made any decision. This and other experiments prove that the brain makes its own decisions on a subconscious level, and people only later feel that 'they' have performed a conscious decision. It

means that we go through life thinking that, unlike the blessedly autonomous operations of the heart and kidneys, a lever-pulling 'me' is in charge of the brain's workings. Libet concluded that the sense of personal free will arises solely from a habitual retrospective perspective of the ongoing flow of brain events. (Berman and Lanza 2010, 38)

The choosing self in the brain is neurologically not as it seems. Similarly, if we practice self-inquiry and ask questions such as "Who am I?", common reports are that no self is found. Just as the idea of me appears as an afterthought in tests, the idea of me is recognized to be just that, an idea. And it's an idea that is constantly evolving in relation to itself and other phenomena.

Yet, paradoxically, as mysterious and nonexistent as it is, your self is unique; there is no one exactly like you.

Look at your fingertips. Look at your eyes in the mirror. No other body in the entire world has the same look.

We see this uniqueness at the heart of oneness. Upon awakening to impersonal, unitive consciousness, everyone expresses it a little differently. The Buddha says it very differently from Jesus Christ. Ramana Maharshi's flavor is quite different from Jiddu Krishnamurti's. You might emphasize the emptiness of self, the nothingness; I might emphasize the fullness, the presence. (And on another day, vice versa!)

While every wave is water, each wave breaks unlike any other.

Exercise: Becoming the Hero of Your Journey

Building on the meditation earlier in this chapter, you are going to explore your life once again, with the specific intent of becoming a hero—not necessarily plucking children from burning buildings or having special powers but simply recognizing yourself as the leading role in this story of your life and honoring the heroic qualities you have displayed. Keep a particular eye out for times in your life when you have displayed courage, bravery, endurance, kindness, nobility, transcendence, generosity, creativity, initiative, determination, tenacity, persistence, discipline, self-control, and so on. You may be more accustomed to identifying the times you have lacked the qualities of a hero, and this balances your view of how you have lived your life.

In *The Hero's Journey*, Joseph Campbell (1990) famously outlined the meta-narrative, the essential story structure that can be applied to every myth and fable throughout human history across cultures. The book has become a framework of screenwriting, and just about every movie you have seen since has been written with this structure in mind. You may like to familiarize yourself with the twelve stages of the hero's journey and look out for the parts of your life that move through them.

The exercise is much like the meditation but using a journal. Allow yourself thirty minutes. For this exercise, write in the third person. By way of example, I might write:

Will Pye was born in Royston, England, in May 1979. A month late, he was a big and heavy baby and in good health. Following a morning delivery, his father and mother brought him home to the recently renovated home with the brown carpet in the lounge and wooden beams throughout. His sister was a little uncertain about this new appearance, yet was kind in her curiosity toward her new friend.

At one year old, he was a little less chubby and beginning to grow blond hair. He held his toy dog close to him and would strongly protect his friend from anyone... and so on.

On completing the exercise, reflect upon the following:

What did you discover about yourself and your life that you were previously less aware of?

What aspects of your uniqueness were revealed through the life review meditation and exercise? How does it feel to celebrate them?

How does choosing to see yourself as a hero of a story create a change in how you feel about you and your life?

What clarity emerges about how you want to show up to the next chapters of your life?

How will recalling your heroic nature, and the epic nature of your human life, affect your life experience moving forward?

Does regarding yourself as a hero from a third-person perspective make it a little easier to feel gratitude for your unique self?

Being Uniquely Divine

Hopefully it is becoming clearer how unclear we are on what the person is, on what self is. We have looked at some ways that the nature of self can be regarded and also at a central mystery: How is it that you are you, both wave and ocean simultaneously, both self and awareness of self?

We have looked at how your life, and any human life, can be viewed as heroic, and how this changes our experience of who we are.

We have explored, too, the overarching truth of the paradoxical mystery within a mystery: how you are patterned, conditioned, just like everyone else, yet at once entirely unique.

For me, this evokes a sense of awe and wonder for the whole of creation, including myself. It gives access to a kind of cosmic view from which I can access a profoundly deep level of appreciation for myself. Recognizing my uniqueness and the uniqueness of each life story allows me to experience greater love for myself and others.

It even offers a tantalizing view of the human being as the means—or at least one means—by which an ever-expanding universe evolves and explores itself. Within this view, the inherent worth and value of myself and every single human being alive is celebrated and enjoyed. A feeling of gratitude for the entirety of creation and every human life throughout eons, including my own, wells up in my heart. A great gratitude for the beingness or being that we all are, and the singular, unique human that I and you are, complement each other in a feeling of immense well-being.

As you go about your day today, keep in mind, whether looking in the mirror or at characters encountered in your play of life, our uniqueness. Keep in mind the intrinsic value we each play in our roles supporting life experiencing itself in a multitude of forms. In appreciating our uniqueness, the uniqueness of each of our family members, our work colleagues, and our friends and foes alike, we tap into a unifying quality of humanity.

Thank you.

Chapter 6

Your Mind's Management

As part of my process of transforming body, mind, and thus my experience of life, I practiced a hybrid of martial arts, integrating taekwondo, kung fu, and karate. In one of the first sessions, I was introduced to the bridge position. I was instructed to place my elbows on the floor with my arms straight out in front, legs back, balancing on my toes, and my whole body raised off the ground. Within a few seconds of holding the position, I had thoughts such as *I can't do this any longer,* and *It's impossible to go on*. The instructor, however, encouraged us to keep going. I think it was just one minute, and in this short time, I got a glimpse of how unreliable thinking is. As my practice deepened, I discovered that thoughts of impossibility would continue to present, and that by not paying attention to these thoughts and continuing to experience the discomfort, I could hold this position for ten minutes even though I had decided it was just too much to bear after thirty seconds.

Similarly, when we begin meditating in a sitting position for thirty minutes or more, we will likely experience strong uncomfortable sensations, probably in the knees or back, and thoughts such as *This is painful, I must stop*, or some variant. However, once again by experiencing the discomfort and staying with the sensation rather than following the thoughts, we develop insight as the "pain" becomes something else, a different type of sensation. We may continue with the meditation and some considerable time later complete it with no more trouble from these sensations.

Through the bridge position and meditation, I discovered just how unreliable the mind is and how conditioned it is to react to discomfort by guiding us away. This is clearly an intelligent function but a very basic part of the mind's operating system. If we want to accomplish anything significant, whether developing a strong meditation practice, completing a degree or book, or integrating our emotional wounding or suffering, we need to learn to transcend the mind. Particularly, we need to learn to disregard its intelligent yet potentially unhelpful reaction away from feeling bad or uncomfortable.

Exercise, meditation, and cold showers are a few examples of the many ways that we can encounter this basic part of our intelligence and get used to moving beyond it. In each case, there will be a mental and bodily reaction away from strong sensation. In each instance of this, we have the simple opportunity to remain with it and in so doing activate and utilize higher functioning of mind and brain. We can give ourselves the experience of being master of our mind rather than its victim. Gratitude is also a powerful way to dissolve or disengage this conditioned reactivity to discomfort. In previous chapters, we have familiarized ourselves with ways we can create a more positive mind-set, perspective, and thus experience of reality. Gratitude balances the negativity that arises in the mind, ultimately replacing it. Once we are familiar with this feeling or vibration, we can apply it to our most resisted emotional pain or discomforts. I recall well the moment in which for the first time I turned to face that knot of energy I called depression and said, "Thank you." The alchemical power of gratitude can be discovered in such moments. What was very bad becomes neutral or even good as a part of me that was being resisted becomes welcomed and loved.

The cultivation of awareness and spaciousness is essential to the managing of mind through gratitude, as is recognizing this basic choice to be conscious master rather than passive victim. The following affirmation reminds us via the mind to be master rather than victim.

Affirmation: *"I am the loving operator of my mind."*

This mental reminder engages the mental body to recognize that we exercise some influence over the type and quality of thinking happening in our awareness. The very act of repeating this ten or so times confirms this through our experience. At the least, we can choose to believe a thought or not.

Repeat to yourself, *I am the loving operator of my mind.* What do you notice?

Be aware of sensations. How does it feel as you repeat this?

Take a minute or a few to further experiment and see how it is for you to hold this particular thought.

Of course, this is the perfect response to a mind of very negative thoughts. By negative thoughts, I mean any thoughts that undermine our well-being, efficacy, and integrity. So, a thought criticizing myself, a guilty or shameful thought, a self-loathing thought, or actually any thought other than simply dealing with the particular error or mistake (if there has even been such an occurrence!) would be a very common example of negative thinking, which many of us are affected by at some point.

A deep breath and the thought, *I am the loving operator of my mind,* immediately point us to the preferable kindness of tone in our self-talk and the potential to choose a different thought or at least to shift awareness away from the undesirable thought. It reminds us and allows us to observe our agency. It ultimately evokes the experience of being a loving observer of thoughts rather than the passive victim of them and the painful feelings they unnecessarily lead to.

As with all the affirmations in this book, use and play with this affirmation with curiosity and the intent to discover for yourself how it is to hold and begin to believe such a thought.

Even if you have encountered a particular affirmation before (the one above is a classic one from the human potential movement), how does it feel to engage with it now?

You may notice if you have played with it previously that it is now far easier to hold in mind and believe. It is very helpful to notice how far you have come in your human journey.

Of course, when it comes to mastering the mental body and using it as necessary, rather than being swept along by conditioning and the collective noise, the perspective that you are the awareness of thinking with the ability to think differently is fundamental. The affirmation, *I am the loving operator of my mind,* is a route out of the mind, using the mind!

Meditation: Noticing and Becoming the Gap Between Thoughts

Perhaps the most common unhelpful thought that arises when we begin to practice meditation is that some variant of thinking is bad, undesirable, or should not be happening. This creates tension and more thoughts. So, though it is pointing to a deeper truth of the stillness and silence of just being, it can obstruct our experiencing this for ourselves. We first must be able to be present witnessing thoughts before they subside. In this meditation, we are going to actively work with thoughts and discover the spaciousness each thought is surrounded by.

Find a comfortable position with your back straight in a place where you will not be disturbed for a period of time, fifteen minutes perhaps.

Begin with a couple of deep breaths to bring attention into the body and into the present moment.

When thoughts arise, simply notice them. (If upon sitting, there are no thoughts for more than thirty seconds, you may want to skip this meditation, for you have accomplished what this meditation can lead to.)

As each thought falls away, notice the space just after it.

Notice the space just before a thought.

Continue to observe how thinking happens, with particular curiosity for the gap between thoughts.

Focus on the gap; become curious about this gap between thoughts.

Notice that the gap widens the more curious you become.

See that the more attention you pay to the gap, the easier it is to be aware of this space as well as the thoughts.

Continue to give attention to the time between thoughts, no matter how little a duration it appears.

When the opportunity to notice the time between thoughts naturally presents, dwell for as long as you can there.

Notice and enjoy this intimacy with spaciousness.

On completing the meditation, ponder what you have discovered. It may be helpful to see that whatever the degree of busyness of your mind, no matter how hectic thought gets, it brings with it spaciousness. And you can expand and cultivate this spaciousness through your curiosity, attention, and practice. It may also be helpful to remember that thoughts are not a problem, that a busy mind can be a necessary and functional part of living a happy and productive life, and that this is most true when you regularly pause and drop into the space between thoughts. Perhaps you may even experience a sense that what you most deeply are is that space and spaciousness.

Free Will? At Least Free Won't

In chapter 5, we encountered the pioneering work of Benjamin Libet and how his experiments suggest our commonsense idea of "me" or the self may be somewhat illusory. Many have interpreted his data to disprove the very idea of human beings having free will. Libet's own interpretations were a little different and can help us understand a key function of our mind's management.

In a 2003 *Journal of Consciousness Studies* paper, Libet used the idea of "free won't." This acknowledges the considerable number of unconscious and involuntary thoughts that come into our mind while emphasizing our ability to disregard, disbelieve, or let them go.

As an example of the variety and volume of thoughts that come into our minds, this morning, as I wrote this book, before I got into a more flowing state of creativity where being and doing unite, all of the following thoughts arose: *This book is so beautiful and unique. This book lacks originality. The writing here is really good; I am a good writer. The writing here is not so good; I am not such a good writer.*

Clearly the mind is, as with determining whether I can hold the bridge position any longer, unreliable here. Its strength, the capacity to take multiple perspectives, is also its weakness. The offering of such a variety of possible truths makes it a challenge to determine what is true for us in the current moment. We can, of course, always change our mind and believe something different on another occasion. Indeed, we might define a "belief" as a thought that we have held to be true repeatedly such that it ultimately becomes an unconscious aspect of how we view and experience life.

Applying Libet's idea of free won't, we can look at part of our mind's management as simply choosing whether to believe a thought that arises or not. We can simply reject those thoughts that are unhelpful, dysfunctional, and go against a core belief or direction we have decided to go in. For example, if I have decided to complete ten minutes of bridge, my job becomes to ignore all thoughts saying I cannot continue. We can extrapolate this to apply to any endeavor such as a marathon, degree, or marriage. Another example might be that we decide to love ourselves, to offer our own being the kindness, respect, and appreciation that we give to others. Now my task becomes simply to disregard, question, ignore, and perhaps replace with better ones all those thoughts that do not align with the intention.

Though this requires willingness, awareness, and diligence, you may notice the liberating aspect of the sheer simplicity of believing this thought or not, one thought at a time. Of course, a meditative practice that slows down the thought stream will be a great help in successfully accomplishing this.

A useful resource for this is Byron Katie's The Work (n.d.), where four simple questions are offered as a framework that expands on the idea of free won't.

1. Is it true?

2. Can you absolutely know that it's true?

3. How do you react, what happens, when you believe that thought?

4. Who would you be without the thought?

A final step is the turnaround. Having examined the thought through the four questions, we look for the turnaround. For example, I may have thought, My *friend is aloof and not a very good friend.* I try on the thought, *I am being aloof and a poor friend.* I see if this is true and discover that indeed, in perceiving aloofness, I become aloof! The turnaround is a great way to discover how we project our own feelings and behaviors onto others. When we see this, we are able to withdraw our projections and see others and ourselves more clearly.

Exercise: Allowing the Mental Body to Re-cognize Your Beauty

Having become the hero of our journey in the last chapter, we are going to continue to adjust and upgrade our thinking mind, the mental body, through becoming aware of thoughts that are particularly unhelpful and replacing them with more helpful thoughts. We are going to "re-cognize," to change our cognition.

An example of a very unhelpful thought would be one that I gave in the first chapter, *I am a f*#king idiot.* It is unhelpful because it affirms and evokes the very qualities I would like to be free of, and like any regularly held thought, it has the potential to become a belief and be self-fulfilling. It is also unhelpful for the simple reason that it feels terrible to believe such a thought. So, what might be an alternative thought about myself that would affirm and evoke the qualities I desire to bring into the world and feel good? One I worked with for some time was simply, *I am love, and all is well.* I encourage you to "try it on" and see how it feels. (We will revisit this affirmation in chapter 10.) Keep in mind that a new thought can be like a new pair of shoes in that it takes a while for it to feel comfortable and be a true fit.

For this exercise, I invite you to consider your view of yourself and your view of the world, and in each instance, identify one to three thoughts that appear regularly in your consciousness. The example above is of course of a view of self. An example of your view of the world could be something like *Life is difficult*, or *Life is unfair*. In each case consider how functional the thought is and how it feels, and then feel into a replacement that is more functional and feels better.

With a blank sheet of paper, work through it like this:

Select one to three thoughts a) about self and b) about the world that don't feel great and are less than optimally functional.

Working with each thought, find an alternative, perhaps using the turnaround method.

Set the intention to utilize this new thought or set of thoughts to be key foundational elements of your new operating system.

Write or type the thought(s) and leave them somewhere around your home or possessions where you will be regularly reminded. Consider setting a reminder on your phone where a daily message pops up.

From Victim to Master

One of the very first insights of meditation is that the mental body is incessantly active. The direct encounter with the degree to which thinking thinks, involuntarily and unnecessarily, is often used *by the thinking* as a reason not to meditate! I often hear from people who have just begun to meditate, "I cannot meditate; my mind is too busy." This is akin to saying, "I cannot exercise because I am too unfit." In each instance, we are learning a skill and developing a capacity that takes practice. Just as that first trip to the gym can be painful and confronting, so it is that our initial attempts to meditate can be off-putting. As the physical discomfort is evidence of the need for exercise, the mental agitation demonstrates a need for some kind of meditation. Just as after a week or two of regular exercising, we notice both increased good feeling and a greater ease of completing what was previously challenging, our meditation practice yields improvements as our regular investment of time yields returns.

If we can see that most action begins with a thought or is at least accompanied by a thought supporting or justifying it, we grasp the importance of developing the capacity to be aware of the thought stream rather than lost in it. When we observe that most thoughts are unhelpful, dysfunctional, and unnecessary—such as worry or labeling everything or everyone we see—we see clearly the value of and need for cultivating a conscious relationship with our mental body.

In practicing being aware of the thinking mind through meditation, we can deepen the realization—or "real-eyesation"—that we are that which is aware. Simply being here now becomes possible. As we practice further, this becomes possible even in otherwise stressful or tense situations. It is as if each time we meditate, we are adding to a reservoir of calm and spaciousness that we then carry around with us, ready to be accessed whenever necessary. In the modern world, especially if we have children, have a mortgage, drive a car, or just have an otherwise full life, it may be necessary several times a day!

A fully mature practice will yield such experiences as the full absorption in the object of attention or awareness itself, such that thinking, including all the self-referencing thoughts, drops away entirely. Turning away from the busy mind is in effect giving it more power to continue dominating your consciousness. Being willing to be with it is the beginning of becoming master of the thinking mind. With the increased spaciousness and slowing down of the thought stream that naturally and somewhat effortlessly unfold when we sit regularly, we now have the opportunity to become manager and ultimately master of the thinking mind. We become able to use the mind rather than be used by it. We become able to access the very silence and peace that we sought when we first sat down to meditate only to discover noise and turmoil.

We may feel tremendous gratitude for our brain and whole nervous system as we discover it is inclined toward peace and balance. This gratitude may expand as we realize "sitting down, shutting up, and not moving"—the most fundamental meditation instruction—is a reliable path for most to step into a more masterful relationship with the thinking mind. With this we can begin to tap into our creative power.

Thank you.

Chapter 7

Your Creative Power

Every cause has an effect, and this is true of each thought, feeling, emotion, intention, and belief we hold in our consciousness. Our consciousness is causative. The body is the perfect playground to experience this truth directly. In my final year of school, I had an important essay to complete and began to notice the early signs of a cold or infection coming on. In an unusual display of commitment to my schoolwork, I resolved not to become ill because if I were to allow illness, I would surely be unable to complete it within the deadline. Though I took some physical measures—drinking lots of water, taking vitamin C—the essence of my response was simply to think and be well. When I felt signs of illness, such as a tickly throat, I thanked my body for being such a wonderfully healthy body and appreciated its capacity to deal with pollution, germs, or viruses. I decided to be healthy and acted like I was. I remained healthy for the three weeks or so that I was working on the paper and was able to hand it in on time. Curiously, once I had done so, I soon became very ill and was bedridden with a fever for several days. It seemed that there had been the conditions of illness within me over the three weeks, yet through will, intention, awareness, and genuine appreciation of the sought-after future outcome being here now, I had created at least a delay. This was all I had sought to create: to remain healthy to complete the work. Perhaps if I had been clear that I wanted to create health, the body would have found a way to process the condition without needing the fever, phlegm, and bed rest!

Not long after this, I left school and was working as a bartender in a busy Cambridge bar. I generally enjoyed the work. Though an introvert, I excelled in the fast-paced environment, enjoyed learning the various cocktails, and would often outperform even the waiters with sales. However, one night, I was feeling very low and did not want to work. Having started my shift, I decided to state my condition to my manager as being a physical one: that I was unwell and could not work. She asked how I was unwell, so I described flulike symptoms and tried to appear sufficiently pathetic so she would realize I was not much use and send me home. To my disappointment, she instead suggested that I take a seat in the break room and see if my condition improved. I sat right by the thoroughfare, beside the entrance through which my manager and others could walk at any moment. Thus, it was key to the integrity of my story that I appeared ill at every moment so its falsity would not be exposed. Having started this charade, I now had to see it through, and so my body and mind assumed the posture and feeling state of past occasions when I felt ill. After a couple of hours or so, I convinced my manager that I was still ill, and she reluctantly sent me home. Here's the curious part—having left the bar as I walked out into the night, I noticed I had a blocked nose, a sore throat, aches, and pains, rather like the flu. I had made myself ill by believing I was and acting as if I was—a lesson in both the folly of dishonesty and the power of mind.

A third similar occasion happened when I was at work in Melbourne, Australia, in my twenties. Seven of us worked in a fairly small space, and five had come down with a nasty and persistent flulike illness. The two of us who had not contracted the condition had been exposed to it frequently. One evening, reflecting on this, a colleague said half-jokingly, "Looks like it's you and me next!" I reacted, "Yeah, right!" As I did so, I realized what I was saying and corrected myself, saying something like, "Actually no, my body is good. I will leave it to you guys!" I resolved to stay healthy, took lots of vitamin C, drank lots of water, and consciously chose to perceive any symptom-like phenomena as evidence of my body creating health and balance. The next day, my colleague called in sick, while I remained the only one of the seven not to contract the illness. I believe this was simply because I was the only one who was fully aware of my own creative power and able to take full responsibility in wielding it.

Those three personal experiences demonstrate the truth of the placebo effect for the majority of human beings, especially for the 30 percent or so that are particularly susceptible. Namely, what we believe is going to happen to our body does happen.

This is one way we can observe our creative power and reclaim our responsibility for our health. This connecting with our capacity to adjust the matter of our physiology offers evidence and a foundation for our capacity to create in the outer world of matter at large. As we can see from the examples above, the intention may be pure or less than wholesome, entirely conscious or a little murky, yet the results are the same. It is this simple yet profound ability to bring into form intricate and complex structures, organizations, and works of art that perhaps sets the human consciousness apart from any other on planet earth. People such as Elon Musk and Oprah Winfrey demonstrate just how creatively powerful a consciously wielded attention, imagination, and awareness can be. If we are willing to dream big, let the universe know what we want, and align our thoughts, emotions, and beliefs to this, the universe will bring forth results often far beyond our imagination.

Affirmation: *"I am a powerful creative being, and I am creating consciously."*

At once empowering and perhaps overwhelming is the recognition that if we are creating through our thinking, feeling, and acting, we are creating in any moment that these are occurring. Thus, our affirmation for the mind here reminds us of this fact. This very moment, we are interacting with the universe in co-creative play. In this context, training our capacity to choose where our attention goes and becoming fully aware of how we think, believe, and feel is crucial. It helps us be at peace, being, doing nothing.

How does it feel to state this: "I am a powerful creative being, and I am creating consciously"? Often it will seem that attention, thoughts, beliefs, and feelings are happening simultaneously, yet in separating them, through close observation, we can break down our process of being such that we can give more attention to each. This way, we are more aware of what is occurring and better able to adjust through reflective awareness. If I had continued to think, *I am a f*#king idiot*, or been unaware of how this mind-set felt, I would not have had the awareness and motivation to change this thought pattern.

As you say the affirmation to yourself, notice how it feels and whether any resistance to the idea of your creative power comes up. You may discover either a feeling of excitement from the empowering aspect or some trepidation from the responsibility this bestows and requires.

Consider how gratitude relates to attention, thinking, feeling, and action and how this binding principle might affect all aspects of our being and thus what we are creating in life. Put simply, if we regularly give attention to aspects of life that we enjoy and appreciate, we will think and feel in appreciation. Our perception and actions are thus likely to follow in the same tone.

With this in mind, try repeating the phrase again. Allow the phrase to generate feelings of gratitude and empowerment.

Meditation: You Are an Energetic Being

It is easier to accept how powerfully creative we are when we realize that we are connected to all phenomena. This way, we can grasp, however rudimentarily, the means by which our thinking, feeling energy body is in communication with the world around us. In chapter 2 we encountered the idea that our heart, our body, gives off a measurable field of electromagnetic energy. Neurocardiology suggests we can influence the quality of this field by affecting the coherence of our heart. Perhaps this explains why in the company of some people we feel peaceful and with others stressed; we may simply be becoming conscious of the quality of their vibrational signal. In my workshops it is often a powerful exercise to walk around a roomful of people with awareness of our energetic field and intending it to be emitting qualities such as peace, joy, and love. Through the idea of our giving off a vibrational signal and this being influenced by what we are feeling and thinking, we can grasp how it is not only our action that is causative but the state of consciousness within which it occurs. Anyone who has played sports can attest to the improved outcome of a swing of a racket or a bat, for example, when in the peaceful, concentrated, and positively expectant state of flow compared to feeling agitated and fearful.

Find a comfortable position in a quiet place and enjoy the following awareness exercise. If you like, listen to its audio track at http://www.newharbinger.com/42020. Take a few deep breaths to bring awareness into the body.

Bring awareness to the palms of the hands and notice what sensations are present. Pay attention to any tingles, warmth, cold, or sense of flow.

Bring your hands together in front of you, palms facing each other, and begin to move them closer to each other and then further away, and vice versa. Does the sensation change as you go from far apart to as close as you can get without touching? Perform all movements slowly and deliberately.

Notice how it is to focus attention on one palm at a time. How does giving more attention or awareness impact the experience of sensation?

Can you feel the same or similar sensations in the soles of your feet?

Switch from palm to palm to sole to sole, giving a minute or so to each.

As you move attention from the center of your palm to the center of your foot, again notice how giving attention affects the depth or intensity of experience.

If you are an experienced practitioner of yoga or qigong, the above exercise will likely seem very basic. Coming into direct contact with our subtle energy system is a natural and direct consequence of such practice. By gaining insight into our energetic nature, we can recognize that everyone else is similarly energetic, as are all phenomena. In this way, we can perceive more clearly how, in adjusting our energetic system through attention, thought, feeling, and action, we are in communication with the world of energy all around and within us.

If We Think and Feel that We Can, We Can

Periods in the history of humanity can be viewed as expressions of the consciousness of humanity at the time or even as a story of one exceptional person who thought very differently. Key historical figures such as Gandhi and Hitler represent extremes of enlightenment and unconsciousness. Consciousness is clearly ethically neutral in this world of duality, of opposites—it seems we can choose to use the power of our minds to create the Holocaust or Indian Independence, to offer two contrasting examples.

How often do you see an elite sportsperson or showbiz star, after lifting the trophy, say, "I have dreamed of this as a child!"? I watched a documentary on the famous chimp expert Jane Goodall. How to explain such an extraordinary life? Luck? A capricious God? Fate? Or the innate creative power of the human consciousness? As Ms. Goodall reflected on her childhood, she said, "All I ever thought about was going to Africa and living with the animals" (Morgen 2017). Another powerful example in recent history occurred when the British athlete, the late Sir Roger Bannister, ran the mile in under four minutes on May 6, 1954. This feat was thought to be humanly impossible. With immense collective effort and top coaching, people had tried and tried and failed and failed. Bannister thought differently and trained differently, and after his success, running a mile in under four minutes became relatively commonplace. Within forty-six days, this timing had been repeated. Within a year, three athletes in one race broke it. To date, over 1,400 athletes have run the distance in under four minutes (Daley 2018; Phillips 2018).

Our thoughts, and those persistent thoughts we call beliefs, influence how we feel about any scenario, and all this together is causative in how an event might unfold. There is perhaps no greater gift a parent can give a child, in terms of beliefs, than "You can do anything you put your mind to."

Let's now look at an exercise to bring us into awareness of what we think and believe and how to create new thoughts and beliefs. This came to me in my darkest hour as a suicidal young man and was a key ingredient within my transformation into a thriving and content human.

Exercise: Creating Your Self

For this journaling exercise, find a quiet place and give yourself as much time as you need. You are going to write a new story of who you are by applying the principle of gratitude for the good to your own story of self.

If you are like most people, you are more critical of yourself than others and might be more inclined to see your faults and imperfections rather than celebrate your qualities and beauty. This can be a functional part of development as you identify your areas of growth. The problem with this, apart from causing you to feel bad—depression usually involves some form of self-attack—is that you conform to your beliefs about who you are. Thus, a negative story of who you are creates precisely more of what you would wish to no longer be.

I encourage you to approach this exercise with a sense of fun and playfulness.

Begin by writing "I am..." and then continue to own, affirm, and celebrate the many qualities of you. Using the present tense is important.

Be brave. Include qualities that perhaps you don't yet 100 percent embody but have shown and wish to exhibit more and more.

Consider what friends and family say about you in the positive yet make sure to truly, deeply feel your appreciation for yourself.

Play big and use your imagination. Don't let confused ideas about what humility is or false modesty obstruct you from affirming your best you.

Here is an example of a perfectly acceptable and good attempt: *I am a courageous and kindhearted human capable of kindness. I am thoughtful and considerate. I am tenacious and persevere when I believe in something. I am intelligent and willing to apply myself to personal growth.*

And here is an attempt that indicates a developed awareness of the creative power we possess and a capacity to really let in the love: *I am an infinite and eternal being with profound gifts as a communicator. I am dedicated to the well-being of others and committed to actualizing my most beautiful and impactful self in service of love and truth. I am generous, kind, and enthusiastic and have an awesome sense of humor. I am a beautifully unique expression of the divine. I am love.*

It may take some practice! For the true magic of this process to be realized, do the following:

Do this exercise every day for twenty-eight days.

Type and print out the ones you like as you go along.

Start afresh every day, using different words, appreciating a variety of qualities, while revisiting and repeating those aspects of who you are that feel especially powerful.

Focus on how your story makes you feel.

Take a moment to give thanks for your ability and willingness to grow and evolve.

Becoming Conscious of Your Creating

Being creative is clearly a defining trait of the human being. Whether singing, writing, sculpting, composing, or building houses, careers, or families, we create. We do so through the primary lens we hold of who we are and what our world is. If I do not believe I can write a book, I will not try. If I believe that I have to work hard to make money, I am unlikely to embrace the opportunity that looks "too good to be true." These are two simple examples. Of course, if I believe I am a victim of life or that it is all fate/luck/God/randomness, I am going to in effect abdicate my power as a creative being.

Our thinking, feeling, and believing in our own creative power is our taking our seat upon the throne of our own consciousness. However, this is made a little trickier by much of our programming, our beliefs, and our being unconscious. Thus, some form of shadow work is necessary whereby we make these unseen elements of how we perceive, and thus create, the world conscious. We must first become aware of what programming we are running if we want to upgrade. It is beyond this book to go into depth around specific methods of such work; however, we can look to the life we have created and how we experience day-to-day reality to give us clues. If, for example, I am always feeling short of time or money, it is likely I have some programming running. If I am strongly reactive to people I perceive as arrogant or angry, I am likely carrying arrogance or anger that I am being called to become conscious of and own. It's not just the darkness that can be repressed or that we can be disassociated from. If I become obsessed with the peace, presence, or confidence I perceive in another, I am likely being called to see these qualities in myself, to see my own light. Wherever there is a strong push or pull showing up consistently, it is likely a reflection of something that needs to be resolved within. Becoming aware of this ongoing creativity via perception, we will naturally choose to make gratitude a habit.

Practicing gratitude for your life and its aspects, and for yourself, creates a grateful brain and mind. This is the most impactful key to transforming your life that I am aware of. You are creating all the time through attention, thinking, and feeling. Create consciously! Create gratefully!

Thank you.

PART 3

How Gratitude Transforms Suffering and Struggle

Chapter 8

Transcending the Limitations of Egomind

The bell rang. Following several years of practicing meditation, I was now several days into a meditation retreat in Colorado in 2009. What was remarkable was that there was no remarking; there was just the bell ringing, no "me" hearing the bell. The commentary and personalizing of experience ceased. It was experienced that there is no one here. There was in fact an emptiness, a selflessness. I realized that I am loving presence. A thought soon followed that the concept of *I* was experienced as just that, an idea. From that point on, I ceased writing a personal journal for some time as it was clear it was a made-up story about a made-up character!

The idea of you and me, of self, is created, and exists only in thought and in relationship with other objects. This is egomind in a nutshell: self-referencing thought. It occurs in the awareness that you are. It typically perpetuates itself through circular loops of negative thoughts about itself, through fearing a future, ruminating on past events, or occupying awareness through the resistance of present-moment emotion, feeling, or sensation. The introduction of authentic appreciation interrupts these loops. Gratitude is the cessation of egomind.

As a child, we had two dogs, both black Labradors. For my first seven years, we had Polly. When Polly died, I can clearly recall my mother, sister, and I hugging in a ball of grief after the news. Gypsy was next and would be my dear friend for ten years. I have never experienced such a pure and uncomplicated love affair as that which Gypsy and I shared. My intention here is not to draw attention to the unbounded love we experience with our pets—though by all means tap into *that* gratitude—but to look at a curious behavioral trait of both Gypsy and Polly that offers a helpful metaphor for egomind.

Ego is a functional part of the operating system that comes with a body. It is the simple and invaluable sense of self that naturally and necessarily accompanies physicality. It allows for all manner of valuable aspects of the human experience, such as relationship, automated avoidance of walking out in front of buses, and so forth.

Egomind refers to the dysfunctional aspect of this operating system that reifies our identity in thought and in time. Its common qualities of misperception are interrelated:

Separation: From other people, from the apparently outer world, from life itself, and from our common source and creator

Materialism: Both ethical, the belief that more stuff will bring more happiness, and ontological, the belief that matter is what matters because it is what reality is made of

Insufficiency or lack: The belief that there is not enough for everyone, leading to competition and comparison, and that I am not enough or that I am unworthy, wrong, or faulty

The fundamental problem with all these beliefs is that they are illusory. They are false. There is no separation, no division, no disconnection; all is literally one. Stuff does not make us happy; studies show that beyond a basic income sufficient for food, shelter, education, and leisure time, we become no happier with more money and stuff. Reality is immaterial being or consciousness. This is a realization available within any nervous system that can be known directly. It is also a conclusion that science is slowly but surely marching toward as the anomalies of the reductive materialist model stack up and fresh thinking emerges. And finally, the nature of nature is plenty. We have had to work very hard to create scarcity. Likewise, every human being is enough, drowning in love. Only the egomind obscures this until it does not, initially via its transformation and ultimately via its transcendence.

Which brings me to Polly and Gypsy. They chased their own tail. It was funny to witness the unbridled innocence and enthusiasm on display. Egomind is much the same. We notice depressed energy and depressing thoughts arise (such as *I* have *depression*, or *I* am *depressed*, rather than *There* is *depression*). Similarly, we notice anxious energy and anxious thoughts arise (such as *I* have *anxiety*, or *I* am *anxious*, rather than *There* is *anxiety*). Or we notice self-loathing, guilt, or a shameful feeling, and self-loathing thoughts arise. Perhaps we notice ungrateful energy, and ungrateful thoughts arise!

Can you see how this is rather like a dog chasing its own tail? The harder it chases, the quicker its prey runs away! The good news is that the simple and natural responses to the dog's folly—awareness and amusement—are helpful responses when egomind is activated.

In awareness, we can begin to actually *feel* the energy, and integrate the feelings through *feeling* them unconditionally, rather than seeking escape in thought, just as the dog chases its tail in a self-defeating vicious cycle.

In seeing the amusing aspect of this, we get the joke. We see the essential humor of the human condition, the idea of you and me as being ultimately true. In laughter, the sort of gentle, loving laughter at our dear dog, we are transcending. We are *seeing* the idea of me rather than *being* the idea of me. In experience, this translates, for example, to being aware of sadness, to feeling sadness rather than *being* a sad person. The former is fluid and more accurate than the latter.

We can even feel grateful for egomind and how its short-term dysfunction is actually functional in the longer-term arc of our development as humans. The self-defeating nature of egomind prompts us to meditate, to inquire, to take action, to lessen our dysfunctions and suffering, and ultimately to experience ourselves as amused awareness. (We will look more at the purposeful nature of suffering in the next chapter.)

Affirmation: *"I am that which is aware. I am loving awareness."*

Before, between, beyond, and within every fearful thought, every identification, is the perfect peace and total stillness of our true nature, awareness. Awareness remains precisely as it is, whether there is pain or pleasure, a "positive" thought or a "negative" thought. The sense of self, who we *think* we are, comes and goes. It is silenced, entirely absent in the present moment of direct relationship with phenomena. Look at what happens when a car backfires, an intense orgasm is experienced, or a book is read. There is just the sound, the bliss, or the reading. Then "me" pops up and says, "That startled me," "I have never had an orgasm like that," or "I am going to stop reading now." Similarly, at night we die, to be reborn in our dreams, and then upon awakening in the morning, we say, "I am awake." You may notice how almost all of the above is nonessential. The self-identity creates itself through all this commentary.

We can see that the sense of self creates itself in time and thought. While the sense of self and all sensation, all phenomena, are transitory, there is an aspect of any experience that is always just as it is. "It" is strictly speaking not an it but a vast subjectivity. It is the vast subjectivity experiencing all phenomena. In meditation, we are practicing being this—what we already are!

Forgive me if this baffles the mind a little. However, language is, like time and thought and a sense of self, something that arises within awareness and therefore cannot contain awareness. Just as you cannot bite your own teeth, you are unable to grasp that which is always grasping with what it is grasping!

It's important to note that realizing awareness can become a strategy of the egomind to avoid feeling or facing that which is deeply uncomfortable. The miracle of gratitude is not about bypassing our human experience, disassociating from it, or placing a veneer of positive thinking over feeling awful. It is more about discovering the ease, peace, and beauty when we directly and fully feel and face life. In this way, it is important to bring awareness into the body and into the center of the heart. Thus, in this affirmation, we emphasize not just the transcendent awareness but the feeling heart. While awareness can very usefully allow us to rise *above* life's intensity, openhearted awareness allows us to move *through* life's intensity, as love.

Play with this phrase and, as ever, be aware of how it feels. Check in with how your head, heart, and gut feel when you say, "I am that which is aware. I am openhearted awareness."

You may discover that this utilizes the mental body, thinking, to bring you into a direct experience of an identity deeper than thought. You may notice that gratitude naturally arises here, without effort.

Meditation: Notice Phenomena, Notice Noticing

Find a quiet place where you will not be disturbed and put aside twenty minutes.

For this meditation you are going to focus on what sounds like two activities: the noticing of phenomena and the noticing itself. It is helpful to separate them into two for the purposes of instruction, and yet you may notice that this division into subject and object is in fact merely conceptual, and not part of your direct experience.

Begin with a few deep breaths to help bring you into this moment. Whereas typically you might seek to hold attention on the breath or a word or sensation, for this exercise let the mind wander. Begin with visual sense phenomena: objects in the room. As you notice them, see how it is to also notice the noticing; be aware of awareness.

Repeat this with sounds, then sensations in the body, and then feelings or emotions that may be present. In each case, allow the curiosity of awareness to fall upon the object and then bring that same curiosity to the awareness.

Reflect upon how easy or difficult this exercise is. Was it more or less so with sights, sounds, sensations, or feelings?

You can play with this exercise anytime.

Consciousness Beyond Life

In the above meditation, you inquired into the true nature of your experience. As with any meditation, you opened to the possibility of realizing or knowing yourself in your deepest identity, not as self-identity or subject but as consciousness itself.

Curiously, we are in a time in humanity's history when the true nature of the physical world is being brought into question. This is happening because of anomalous data that cannot be explained within the view of reality that we have long believed. The belief system of reductive materialism— the idea that we are living in a world of separate things that can be broken into ever smaller parts and that we and the world are primarily physical beings—is crumbling. As we peered deeper into the quantum, we discovered that in fact, there are no facts, no things, nor any material to reduce. At the core there is probability or possibility. Furthermore, we discovered that the probability of a particular possibility presenting itself in any moment is affected by consciousness. The observing immaterial consciousness is a cause of which matter is an effect. This truth is so challenging that 100 years after its initial discovery, science is still grappling with finding a worldview that incorporates the complementary truths of Newtonian and quantum mechanics into a unified view. Yet as reality reveals more of itself, we are compelled by yet more anomaly to revise our view and include consciousness as primary and fundamental to the arising of everything.

One particular anomaly is that of the survival of consciousness beyond death. Under the reductive materialist belief system, this is impossible; consciousness is posited as an illusion or an epiphenomenon of brain activity. However, subjective reports such as *Dying to Be Me* by Anita Moorjani (2012) and *Proof of Heaven* by Dr. Eben Alexander (2012) and research into near-death experiences or NDEs are demonstrating that although the brain, heart, and rest of the body can die, an individual consciousness can remain aware. *Consciousness Beyond Life* by Dutch cardiologist Pim van Lommel (2010) is perhaps one of the best summaries of this field and includes a debunking of the attempts by believers in materialism to squeeze this anomaly into their worldview.

This changes everything. Indeed, Alex Tsakiris says as much in his book *Why Science Is Wrong…About Almost Everything* (2014). He argues that science is wrong about almost everything but particularly about the reductive materialist view and the dismissal of the relevance of subjective states of consciousness. If consciousness is primary and causative, then the qualities of consciousness we experience take on a new importance. The power of gratitude can be more fully recognized.

I feel immensely grateful to be alive in this time of shifting paradigms, a time in which we are revising the most fundamental ideas about the true nature of both human beings and the world. We are in the midst of a revolution of consciousness.

Exercise: Life Review from the Perspective of Consciousness

Earlier in this journey, we explored becoming the hero of our own life narrative. In this exercise, we are going to do something similar with a subtle yet important twist. You may wish to use the life outline you created in the earlier exercise for this.

With either the existing timeline or a newly written one, go through your life journey but with an emphasis upon the consciousness rather than the character. Regard your life from the perspective of your deepest timeless identity rather than from merely your ever-changing, time-based self.

To whatever extent you can, come into contact with the continuous core of all experience. Rather than having the experience of consciousness, are you able to feel into what it is like to be consciousness having the experience of you? What changes when you look at it this way? Might this offer a helpful perspective in day-to-day life?

Continuing your inquiry into the nature of your experience, let us consider two things. These may be your direct experience, or for now you may simply consider them conceptually. First, we can see that egomind is not naturally grateful. It is more accustomed to perceiving problems and lack rather than possibility and plenty. Consciousness, on the other hand, may be experienced as naturally grateful.

Thus, gratefulness may be seen as a cause and consequence of awake consciousness. We may discover in our own experience what William Blake (1906) was pointing to when he said, "Gratitude is heaven itself." We may just discover that gratitude is a way to experience the heavenly realization of being undivided, at peace, and at one with the world as consciousness. In so doing, we discover a route into the present moment, beyond egomind and the cessation of suffering.

Realizing You Are an Infinite and Eternal Being

We have looked into how our thinking mind identifies as "me" and how in its self-referencing and resistance to phenomena, it can be likened to a dog chasing its tail. We have considered that the most helpful response to the egomind is similar to how we might respond to a dog chasing its tail: a detached and amused appreciation. We don't need to take ourselves so seriously when we see that we are just a figment of divine imagination.

In this awareness of the egomind, we begin to know ourselves as that which is aware and begin to see how the craziness of the egomind is our prompt to literally look elsewhere. This change in perspective is occurring in more and more people on the planet. It is a natural evolution of consciousness arising as more peaceful being, abundantly present and creative. What a wonderful contribution to our collective growth into the truth of our one human being.

In practicing gratitude, being present with our emotional experience, and witnessing self-referencing thoughts rather than believing that these thoughts define us, we begin to see life entirely differently, from grateful consciousness rather than ungrateful egomind. In the life review exercise, we got a taste for how different it is to experience life as the witnessing presence rather than the character. We can apply this to our day-to-day life and experience life as the naturally peaceful, grateful consciousness. As we shall see in the next chapter, the suffering that often precedes such clarity is not out of place. The egomind and suffering are not errors or wrong but rather necessary states of consciousness, until they are not. They are fuel for our growth into that which is beyond suffering.

In perhaps the ultimate reframe of the suffering and drama of our life story, we have become aware that the essence of who we are in every experience is not dependent upon our body or brain being alive to continue. In seeing that consciousness continues beyond the end of our life, we touch the eternal and infinite nature of our being. Egomind is born, both from the birth of our sense of identity (at around eighteen months) and in each moment through reaction or resistance to an object of awareness as the default-mode network is activated. Similarly, egomind dies both in the cessation of resistance or reactivity through training awareness and in physical death, when the brain and all functions within cease to operate.

What is unborn and does not die is the consciousness that you are.

Thank you.

Chapter 9

The Purpose of Suffering

It is the nature of the human experience, of being embodied, to encounter pain. A wide range of emotional experiences and a body that will hurt, become ill, and eventually die are unifying elements of each human life. While the pain of loss, failure, sickness, old age, and death is unavoidable, suffering is optional. However, typically one must first experience suffering in order to discover this, which brings us to its purpose: its cessation. By being willing to fully experience pain, discomfort, disappointment, loss, grief, and so forth willingly, we come to see that the essence of suffering is resistance to what is. Suffering's cessation is appreciation of what is.

If I look at my life and all the effort and practice I have put into my own transformation, I see that there were two very different yet entirely complementary motivations: the pull of a yearning for truth and the push of wishing to escape my suffering. I tried everything to escape suffering—drugs, alcohol, sex, gambling, and then as I grew up, exercise, meditation, work, and thinking. To be precise, the suffering was an intensely heavy energy in my whole body, centered around my heart. It was characterized by feelings of hopelessness, despair, a strong self-loathing, and a sense of utter pointlessness and futility of life. However, there was one characteristic that preceded and thus colored all the others: resistance.

Resistance is the essential quality of egomind, and it is thus in the releasing of resistance that we release egomind. Here, "my suffering" becomes simply "suffering." Without personal ownership, suffering is transformed. Try saying to yourself, "I am depressed," and "There is a heavy depressed feeling," and note the difference. Is one less depressing than the other? One highly effective way I have found to create this spaciousness around suffering is to face that which you are resisting and to say, "Thank you." This discovery was in many ways the seed for this book fifteen years ago. I see now that through years of resistance and self-centered narratives, I created a demon of sensation and discomfort in my chest. In bowing down—another function of suffering is surely to bring humility—to this pain and truly welcoming it with a thank-you, I began the process of allowing it to be met, loved, and accepted as it is. I learned to be met, loved, and accepted as I am.

The story of the chickpea, a Sufi fable, metaphorically illumines our human predicament and its resolution rather nicely. The chickpea, when placed in the boiling pot, rises to the surface, as if doing all it can to escape the intense heat. With time and encouragement, the chickpea falls into the pot and allows the heat to do its work of transforming it from hard, tasteless, and inedible to soft, slightly sweet, and edible. Perhaps we can see how we are similarly put through trials and challenges and are softened, sweetened, and made more useful by the process.

As I was growing up, I had a deep sense of this process, and it helped me face the challenges of depression, addiction, and the like. In each case, I felt sure that in my working through it, I would be able to help others. This perspective and a quote from a curious source of wisdom were consoling, allowing opening to the pain, the suffering, the heat. The quote is, "The finest steel has to go through the hottest fire," which is attributed to Richard Nixon (1973). Perhaps not a common source of sagely perspective, yet we can assume his own fiery fall from grace yielded insight too.

What I found is that like the chickpea, it is in yielding to the heat that we find freedom. In surrendering to the hopelessness, despair, and challenge, in really feeling and facing suffering head on, saying a big "Yes!" or "Thank you" as necessary, we find release. Simply, suffering is resistance, surrender its cessation, and gratitude the intermediary.

I have found that not only is the end of suffering the purpose of suffering but that specific types of suffering yield specific benefits of wisdom, insight, or opportunity. In this chapter, we will explore how with gratitude we can create this alchemy in real time as the events of our life unfold rather than only with hindsight.

Affirmation: *"This too will pass."*

There is a story of an emperor of old who goes to his wisest counsel, his philosophers, priests, and scientists, and asks them to find the ultimate truth, expressed in one phrase or sentence. After much cogitation, contemplation, and consideration, they return with their conclusion: "This too will pass."

Along with a sense of its purpose, this quote can be of great help when we find ourselves in the midst of suffering. If there is strong emotional pain or a challenging situation, we can remind ourselves of its impermanence. This may create enough space around the intensity such that it softens. Both "Thank you" and "This too will pass" can be blended into an alchemical potion that transforms the lead of suffering into gold.

Of course, "This too will pass" can be accurately applied to everything. Challenging circumstances, intense discomfort, despair, and also very positive states, such as joy, all pass. Just as we resist discomfort, we are inclined to try to hold onto positive sensation. Thus, joy might give way to discomfort, and we may find ourselves both resisting the discomfort and bemoaning the lack of joy. "This too will pass" speaks to our life as a whole. Remembering that this will come to an end can liberate us from complacency or taking it for granted and can prompt appreciation of this moment in which we are alive and well. In coming into contact with the fleeting nature of all phenomena, including our very existence, we access a sweet freedom. As William Blake put it: "He who binds to himself a joy does the winged life destroy. He who kisses the joy as it flies lives in eternity's sunrise" (Gilchrist 1880, 126). The remembrance that all is in constant flux frees us to greet each moment as it is.

Play around with this affirmation. How does it feel? What circumstance in your life right now can it be helpfully applied to? Consider writing this out on sticky notes and placing them around your home, or setting a notification on your phone to remind you regularly.

Meditation: Noticing the Fleeting Nature of Sensation and Sitting with Discomfort

Each of these meditations is designed to facilitate insight into the nature of suffering and the alchemical power of your own presence. One is preparatory, and the other is responsive to moments of intense discomfort or emotion. The second part is also an introduction to breathwork. In each instance, find a quiet place where you will not be disturbed. Download the audio for this exercise at http://www.newharbinger.com/42020.

Part 1: Noticing the Fleeting Nature of Sensation

Begin by bringing awareness into the big toe of your left foot, then moving across the toes to the little toe, along the side of the foot, the sole, around to the ball of the big toe, then to the heel, ankle, and Achilles tendon. Bring awareness into the body by bringing awareness into each part.

Continue scanning through the whole body up the left and right. There is no right or wrong order in which to do this. Start with the intention to bring awareness into every part of the body during the meditation. Twenty minutes should be about right to complete the whole body.

As you encounter stronger sensations—whether in the soles of your feet, in the palms of your hands, as an ache or tension, or as a tingle here or there—allow attention to rest on this stronger sensation. Become curious about the warmth or cool, the feeling of flow or contraction, the mildness or intensity.

Notice how holding awareness on a particular sensation affects it. Does it remain the same? Does it become more or less of the particular quality that you first noticed or does it perhaps become something altogether different?

Part 2: Sitting with Discomfort

This meditation is super simple. When you are experiencing strong emotional discomfort, sit with it.

Rather than using Facebook, a cookie, or thinking to escape the discomfort, take yourself to the meditation mat or your quiet place, set the timer for twenty minutes, and resolve to simply be with the sensation, the feeling, as it arises in the body.

The key thing to keep in mind is that you are not seeking to change the feeling, just to feel it. Of course, you may notice that it does indeed change within your willingness to let it be as it is.

Further to Richard Nixon's wisdom, we can look to other processes in the natural world that evidence the purpose of intense experience. A piece of coal is converted into its energy potential via a slow process of intense compression. Much the same can be said of the diamond—a huge amount of heat and pressure over vast spans of time create an extraordinarily strong and beautiful object.

It is perhaps in the butterfly's metamorphosis that the purposeful nature of suffering is best evidenced in the natural world. The humble chrysalis is the container in which the caterpillar encases itself before dissolving in its own acidic juice. Hardly a pleasant process, one would assume, yet in that process of destruction emerge the seeds of rebirth as a butterfly. Imaginal discs or cells contain the essence of what becomes the butterfly. A similar process of spiritual emergence may be under way within human mental health crises, something we are increasingly becoming aware of. In such instances, it may not be medication but loving presence and a trusting in the messy process that best supports resolution.

Though a thank-you can help us lean into our emotional pain and begin to practice "presencing"—noticing that part within us that needs to be met, loved, and accepted—there may also be much unconscious patterning or defenses that were erected at an earlier age to avoid the intensity and hinder the completion of this process. There is a powerful addition to the sitting with discomfort practice that may be beneficial to help access the root or essence of the suffering and aid the metamorphosis. I encountered this at a Transformational Breath workshop and then in a powerful book that goes into greater depth. Here I share the basic practice of using breath to integrate an emotional charge for you to get started. If you are drawn to dive deeper, I encourage you to seek out either a Transformational Breath practitioner or workshop and/or *The Presence Process* by Michael Brown (2005). For now, we will look at the practice of connected breath. This is conscious breathing in which we remove the pause between breaths. If you look at a dog or cat breathing, you will notice a continuity of inhalation and exhalation. The human is the only mammal that pauses and interrupts the flow of the breath. This practice is to restore the flow. In addition to oxygenating the blood, it develops our concentration practice and occupies the mind such that pains and niggles of our emotional body can rise into presence, into our awareness, and we can experience being accepted and loved.

Find a comfortable posture in a location where you will be undisturbed.

Breathe in and out normally; then begin to do so without the pause. Exaggerate so that you can hear your breathing.

As the out-breath comes to completion, the in-breath is beginning.

As the in-breath is completing, the out-breath is beginning.

While the in-breath requires some effort, as if pushing up, the out-breath can be a release, as though you are letting it fall.

Take care to ensure the in- and the out-breath are of equal proportion to balance oxygen and carbon dioxide levels.

Practice. It might take a little while to gain proficiency—persist and try daily.

Use in response to suffering when a more active engagement feels necessary. Do so with the intention to feel more fully, and to face what is rather than escape.

In the exercise later in this chapter, you will learn a simple technique to help you discover the specific purpose of your difficulties and challenges and how gratitude and curiosity reveal this purpose. Let's first look at the evidence that suffering might be a key ingredient in creating extraordinary lives.

How Some Have Flourished Through (or Because of) Suffering

History is littered with great artists, writers, influencers, and leaders who have suffered intensely. Vincent van Gogh,

Friedrich Nietzsche, Ludwig van Beethoven, Victor Frankl, Frida Kahlo, Jesus Christ, Socrates, and Helen Keller are but a few names that trip off the tongue. As the American author Helen Keller, who was blind, deaf, and mute, noted, "Although the world is full of suffering, it is also full of the overcoming of it" (Keller 1903). She appears to have concluded from her own experience that there is a deeper purpose to suffering and hardship, not just in its cessation or overcoming it, but in qualities or capacities that we can develop only through such initiation and ordeal. Keller noted, "Character cannot be developed in ease and quiet. Only through experience of trial and suffering can the soul be strengthened, vision cleared, ambition inspired and success achieved" (Keller 1938, 60).

I recall having a sense of this when my parents divorced when I was twelve years old. Though a horrible time for us all, I felt that this hardship was functional, purposeful, and a complementary difficulty to the ease of my early years. That I now play the role of spiritual teacher is perhaps due to not much else than the qualification of having suffered intensely, discovered a way to this suffering's cessation, and being naïve enough to hope I can help others in the same process.

The adaptive capacity we are speaking of here is often regarded as humanity's greatest and defining trait. Indeed, is it not life's essential quality, is evolution itself not a process of overcoming dysfunction, hardship, and challenge? The piece of coal, the diamond, the butterfly, the willow that has learned how to bend, all offer powerful examples of how seemingly very bad and wrong phenomena are revealed in time to bring much good and rightness.

As you reflect on the names above and others whom you admire, consider the role suffering has played in their lives. Ask, "Who would they be without their suffering?" to recognize the powerfully purposeful role of suffering. Ask, "How much more did they become by overcoming or transmuting suffering?" to recognize the power of the human spirit to overcome. Reflect on your life and how you have overcome. We will now look at a series of practical steps that will support you in reframing and overcoming, even finding the gift and opportunity in any current areas of your life that you sense are ripe for transformation.

Exercise: The Radical Gratitude Process

The following is a simple means of reframing an exercise that I have shared with hundreds of people around the world in Radical Gratitude Playshops and retreats.

Find a pen and paper and then move through the following steps.

1. Select an issue, emotion, or circumstance that you feel stuck with and wish to explore.

2. Accept that you do not know what it truly means or whether it is "good" or "bad."

3. Ask, "What is the opportunity here?"

4. Ask, "What gift is within the difficulty?"

5. Ask, "If I had somehow created this to evolve and grow greater capacities, what are they?" Think big fish here: What noble quality or extraordinary capacity might this yield? Think of, for example, learning unconditional love rather than speaking another language!

6. How does it feel to create a gift, opportunity, and growth, alchemizing shit into gold?

7. How is your life now enhanced?

The first step can be applied to any circumstance or feeling around which you want to create transformation. The second step is important because having defined the issue by naming it, you are recognizing that there is possibly more to it than that definition. You are making room in your mind for an alternative perspective to emerge. Recall from chapter 1 that all perspectives are equally true and untrue, or partial. This perspective shifting allows you to look at different perspectives that might be more helpful or functional. They might simply feel better.

The three power questions—3, 4, and 5—are designed to do just this. Quite simply, by looking for the gift, opportunity, or great learning, you are vastly more likely to find it.

The final two questions are about integrating this technique into a new worldview, an operating system, through which you will perceive and consciously create your life experience.

Reflect on how your experience of changing the way you looked at an issue changed how you experienced it. Consider that your experience of life is determined not by events but by your perception, the meaning you make. How fundamental and transformational to be grateful!

Alchemizing Suffering with Gratitude

We have seen that as intense, unpleasant, and undesirable as challenge and suffering might be, they have a purpose. This might be an outcome we could not foresee from the level of consciousness with which we first encountered the metaphorical boiling water, and the challenge itself may bring a deep shift in consciousness. From this perspective, we can grasp that suffering's purpose is prompting a beneficial shift in how you live.

We have learned that all phenomena changes, that all intensity subsides, that all emotion moves, that suffering ends.

In the three meditations, we have accessed practices to prepare for, respond to, and transmute suffering.

We have looked at how our view of a circumstance, rather than the circumstance itself, is what determines our experience of the circumstance. We have seen many examples of people who have modeled this in their own lives and learned a simple practice that we can apply to any circumstance to consciously choose a helpful perspective.

We have seen as well that the essence of suffering is contained in resistance to what is, and thus it is in the release of resistance or surrender that suffering ceases. We may just find that we can now love and welcome suffering in excited expectation of the gift, opportunity, and transformation it might yield. In this, we begin to experience a deep relaxation of the nervous system, a relaxing of the fight-or-flight neurology, and a sense that all is well.

It is in this releasing of resistance to suffering that suffering is transformed. Whether by giving a purposeful meaning to challenge or simply yielding to the pain, in ceasing to resist what is, we can open into the freedom from suffering that is our openhearted awareness.

Imagine how life experience alters when we continue to ask, "What is the opportunity here?" If you are experiencing difficulty now, or the next time that you do, may this question offer some relief. If you feel its power, perhaps place it somewhere you will see it regularly.

Thank you.

Chapter 10

All Is Well

We are collectively living a sort of madness, poisoning the air and water that constitute our physical bodies and attempting to create infinite growth within a finite system. We face the very real possibility of creating an extinction of our own species. Our healthcare system is so corrupted by pharmaceutical companies that by conservative estimates it is itself the third biggest cause of death (Starfield 2000). Our economic system intentionally redistributes wealth from the poor to the rich. Our leaders are so corrupted and without courage that they not only let this slide but ignore the will of the people by launching illegal wars to serve the economic interests of their friends' companies. Our media are the very same companies, which explains their inexcusable silence. Relatively, there is so much wrong, so much calling us to act in the world. Yet, abiding in awareness, I feel and know that all is deeply well. It is a paradox for sure—to be in awareness of the immensity of the challenges we face, yet know, feel, and emit the peace and love of all being well, and to act in the world from this place. This is perhaps what a truly sacred activism looks like: inspired by great examples from the past such as Mahatma Gandhi, Rosa Parks, and Martin Luther King, and informed by the latest science that posits us as causative aspects within one unified field of consciousness. We will look at this more deeply in chapter 12.

Every human experiences the trauma of birth—the painful separation from our warm womb of safety. It is easy to see that somatically this is experienced as a rejection of love. Though there are skillful ways of managing this transition to minimize the trauma by sustaining the connection to love and warmth, these are uncommon and generally not available at hospitals. Even with such thoughtful parenting as selecting a water birth, trauma can ensue.

Even if we do somehow escape the pain and separation of birth, we will encounter pain and separation when our parents fail to love us unconditionally. Even the most loving and devoted parents will be unable to maintain a perfect flow of unconditionally loving presence, primarily because their parents did not model this, because their parents' parents did not, and so on. Predictably, the sleep-deprived parent will experience moments of reactivity. Inevitably a human will find sadness, anger, or other natural emotions a child displays to be unlovable when they have yet to love these emotions in themselves. This will be communicated both implicitly and explicitly.

Additionally, genetics will ensure that unresolved trauma from generations prior may manifest in our nervous system. It is the very nature of the nervous system that it has evolved to be highly sensitive to threat. Fear, freeze, fight, or flight was for so long a highly functional operating system.

It is no wonder that we are imprinted with a subtle, or not so subtle, anxiety. I have faced this fear of death, of annihilation, directly when encountering precursor symptoms of a grand mal seizure. As I have shared, a paradoxical surrender and intentional breath—a simultaneous acceptance and action—was my way to discover peace at the core of this anxiety. Perhaps our collective crises invite the same embodiment of loving acceptance and powerful action, that we may create a new world from the clutches of catastrophe. It is no surprise that we will likely find that our nervous system requires recalibrating in order to experience the peace and unconditionally loving presence that it is designed to experience. Ongoing well-being and the experience of love, regardless of circumstance, are our birthrights. The discovery or rediscovery of these may well be regarded as the purpose of our life. To move from fearful body to loving being is clearly an evolutionary edge and offers immeasurable advantage. To *experience* that all is well is a great gift. To be aware of all pain, suffering, and collective crises, and to feel fully and yet ultimately experience peace and love benefits everyone. We must first be willing to feel and pass through all that is not peace.

As a child I would have anomalistic experiences of peace and love. They would pop up out of the blue without apparent cause and serve as oases and a sense of what was possible. This sense was greatly accentuated by ingesting a pill that contained the compound 3,4-methylenedioxymethamphetamine—better known as MDMA, or ecstasy—at the age of fourteen. This gave the experience, for several hours, of unconditional love; love was directed at myself and every other person, without exception. This was, of course, an entirely novel experience for my depressed teenage self and body. I had decided that becoming dependent on a drug to feel good—such as with SSRIs (selective serotonin reuptake inhibitors) or recreational substances—was not a solution to the problem, yet here was a taste of what was possible. It served as relief from suffering and motivation to create this experience for myself as an ongoing reality. Knowing my brain could feel this good, I experimented with how to create such a state naturally. Gratitude and meditation have been my primary tools to accomplish this. However, I will be forever grateful to MDMA for giving such profoundly good, true, and beautiful insight into the nature of the human experience. I may well not be alive if I had not been graced with such a powerful reason to live.

It is not my intention to advocate drug use; quite the opposite, it really depends on the drug and our motivation for using it. I am interested in the education and empowerment of people to make their own free choices. When you know the truth of MDMA, 5-MeO-DMT, psilocybin, CBD, and others, you may find valuable therapeutic use for them at some point. Equally when you know the truth of alcohol, tobacco, and sugar, you may use these drugs less. If you wish to find out more about the medicinal and therapeutic nature of drugs, http://www.maps.org is the site of the Multidisciplinary

Association for Psychedelic Studies while http://www.drug policy.org provides valuable information and perspective. If you wish to understand the harmful effects of pharmaceutical medicines and the fraudulent means by which they are marketed and pushed on consumers, Ben Goldacre's *Bad Pharma* is exhaustive and excellent, while the Cochrane Foundation's work in giving patients and doctors access to evidence of medicines' efficacy and harm is invaluable: http://www.cochrane .org/. When you know the truth of the medicine the doctor is offering you—perhaps by reading and heeding the thousands of words detailing the ways it might cause the condition you hope it will cure or otherwise make you ill—you may find you have less use for it too. Where the law fails truth and justice, our personal intuition and reasoning allow discernment.

I feel deep appreciation for all the organizations and publications, for the many plant spirit medicines, and for MDMA especially. I am grateful that it is once again being studied for its immensely beneficial long-term therapeutic effects.

Affirmation: *"I am love, and all is well."*

Though the experience of all being well is a somatic, felt consequence of the nervous system being supported and coming into balance and harmony, it is useful to have a signifier, as a mental reminder of the state of consciousness in which all is realized to be well. The idea is not the reality, though it can symbolize or evoke the feeling of it, just as a map is only representative of the territory it charts and is designed to help your direct experience of the territory.

"All is well" is not a value judgment. It is not looking at the world and saying the bad stuff—and there is bad stuff—is good; it is looking beyond and above all relative judgment. "All is well" is a felt sense that arises when all that feels off or unwell, every fear, anxiety, and despair, has been fully felt, met, and loved in our own loving presence.

I am love, and all is well.

Try saying this to yourself. Experiment with saying this out loud or silently to yourself, repeating it rapidly or saying it deliberately slowly.

How does it feel to say this?

Can you say it as if you believe it?

How might it feel to truly believe it? Be curious and stay open even if it feels impossible. Pause and contemplate.

Meditation: Taking a Cosmic View

You can likely recall events that seemed to be the end of the world at the time, but looking back, you can now see they were not so important after all. For example, the first time a girlfriend ended a relationship with me—and the second or third!—seemed like the world had caved in. Now I can see it was no big deal. Now, I can see nothing is such a big deal. Let's look at a guided meditation to help us generate this insight. You can download this audio track at http://www.newharbinger.com/42020.

Find a comfortable position in a spot where you will not be disturbed, and begin.

> If you have a particular challenge or issue that you sense you might benefit from gaining perspective on, hold it in mind.

> Take several deep breaths.

> Imagine yourself now sitting in the same spot twenty-four hours later.

> Imagine yourself coming back to this seat one week on.

> Imagine you are now returning to this seat after one year has passed.

> Repeat this for a decade, now fifty years, one hundred years.

> Your life has ended many years ago. How is it to look down at this empty seat and see yourself at this time with the worry or concern you experienced?

> Reflect on what you noticed as your perspective shifted through time.

What communications or helpful perspectives came through? What does your future self say to you now?

Move on 500, 1000, 10,000 years.

3 billion years from now, the sun has exploded…

You get the idea. Ironically, just as we find peace and freedom in the present moment, we can travel in time to broaden our perspective, take a cosmic view, and experience this moment more wisely.

When I share the view that all is well without having the opportunity to dialogue and create understanding of what these words symbolize, a common reaction is often something like this: "How can you say that when the Syrian refugees remain homeless, the displaced people of Palestine suffer violence daily, we are approaching peak oil, water supplies are running out, millions of animals are right now being mistreated, millions of children are being abused, billions live in poverty, and we are approaching species extinction via our own insane interaction with our planet home?" This response assumes I am stating that all that could be improved should be ignored or that it is fine as it is. This is not what I am saying. I am referring to an embodied state in which it is felt and realized that there is nothing to fear. In this state, even death itself may be experienced in trust, peace, and loving presence. I will continue recycling, attempting to minimize my footprint upon planet earth; however, I trust in the vast intelligence of this ecosystem and the vast intelligence of the universe itself.

That said, a look into the relative state of affairs is quite revealing. It suggests we might not even need to take a cosmic view to support the idea that all is well.

Are We Getting Better at Being Human?

In his book *Enlightenment Now* (2018), Canadian American cognitive scientist Stephen Pinker argues that the doom-and-gloom view of our world falling apart is a projection of our psychological biases, not an accurate reflection of the data. He further argues that much of our worldview is formed through the hugely distorting lens of the news media. The focus on the sensational latest armed conflict, posturing dictator, plane crash, or disease outbreak rather than the less exciting deep analysis of statistical trends paints an inaccurate view of what is happening. In presenting seventy-five graphs of multiple measurements of human progress, from infant mortality to the amount of conflict now compared to previous eras, Pinker argues a persuasive case for the idea that in all major measures of human progress such as life, health, prosperity, safety, peace, knowledge, and prosperity, we are doing measurably better than ever. In *Factfulness* (2018), Dr. Hans Rosling, the Swedish international health expert and TED talk sensation, makes a similarly persuasive case. Check out Rosling's most popular and very entertaining TED talk "The Best Stats You've Ever Seen."

Familiarizing myself with both works, I noticed a strong correlation of our collective perspective with individual psychology. We are inclined to perceive a far worse world than the facts indicate. And, while Pinker and Rosling help correct our view of the collective with facts, figures, and graphs, we are also able to correct the bias of our own view by using gratitude.

Here, we touch on the idea that gratitude is not just a way of feeling better, of gaining insight, of integrating our emotions, of reframing challenge as opportunity, or of creating a better relative truth, though it is also all those things. We can consider that the evidence of cognitive science and our own experience support the idea that to be grateful is to align with absolute truth.

This life is a gift. Each breath, our very being, the mystery of our consciousness, is a gift of staggeringly generous proportions. Gratitude is true! "All is well" is true. Such a state of consciousness rather than one of anxiety or fear surely helps how we respond to the problems and challenges we now face. In recognizing that we have come so far and have already overcome so much, we can feel confident in overcoming and resolving the current crises. In clarifying the keys of our success—reason, science, and logic—we are empowered to know what tools to use in the process. In recognizing our interconnectedness as one field of consciousness, we see that our body-mind emanating well-being is the greatest gift we can give back. In being peace, love, integrity, and awareness, we are the change we wish to see. In gratitude we have a practice, a path, and a destination.

Exercise: Seeing Teachers and Teaching Everywhere

I have been very fortunate to access several powerful teachers in my life. My parents are but the beginning of a large number of people who have helped me learn to be a better human. Zen teachers, qigong masters, yogis, hundreds of authors, saints, and masters dead and alive have been hugely influential. I feel immense gratitude reflecting on their impact upon my life.

However, my greatest learnings have come from life itself and the people with whom I have interacted, especially the most difficult or challenging people. From my parents' divorce, to suicidal depression, to addictive behavior, to heartbreak, to illness, these are the times in which my learning has been greatest. Humility, compassion, and insight into the nature of mind are priceless, and I am grateful for all the ways life has delivered these teachings.

In this exercise, you are going to explore how life has taught you. To experience life as a learning opportunity is a powerful way to make peace with your past and be resilient as the journey unfolds.

For this, you will need pen and paper and a quiet place where you will not be disturbed.

Select the three most difficult experiences or times of your life and the three most difficult or challenging people in your life. Write each down. Apply the three power questions from the previous chapter, or the one that resonates most deeply for you, to each circumstance or person.

1. What is the opportunity here?

2. What gift is within the difficulty?

3. If I had somehow created this to evolve and grow greater capacities, what would they be?

As you work through each difficulty or challenging relationship, reflect on any specific learnings and also the theme or themes that might emerge. Keep an eye out for the most valuable qualities or insights such as forgiveness, compassion, resilience, endurance, persistence, kindness, unconditional love, courage, vulnerability, or creativity.

Consider how this perspective helps you navigate life with everyone and everything and is an opportunity to grow and expand. Feel into how grateful you are for this whole human experience.

Realizing Deeper Truth

In this chapter, we have looked at a view of our life and the world as a whole that might be challenging to our existing thought system and emotional body. If we do not *feel* well, then we will likely be challenged by the idea that all is fundamentally okay. However, this shift, essentially from fear into love, from inner division into peace, is possible. We can create well-being and peace if we are willing to do the work, undertake the practice, and choose to be responsible for our experience. We have seen that taking a bigger-picture view and practicing radical gratitude, where we come to appreciate everything that happens as beneficial, allows a moment-to-moment transformation. Learning to love our fear, shame, and despair allows our nervous system to experience peace. We have begun to see that in surrendering to life as it is, in saying yes to life as it is, in being grateful for life as it is, life is experienced very differently. This supports our being agents of change.

That we can create this and that our nervous system is actually capable of feeling good and well, regardless of circumstances, are facts for which we may feel immense appreciation. That our brain, in head, heart, and gut, is responsive to our mind's effort to transform and feel better is surely cause for celebration. Every day is a gift in which we get to start again. Every challenge, difficulty, or painful person is an opportunity to deepen our practice. Throughout this book, and likely throughout our life, we have been learning how to recognize that life is happening for our growth and well-being, to see as it unfolds how it is one big setup, one big conspiracy, to facilitate our personal evolution.

We can also recognize that whatever the beliefs or ideas we may have had about humanity or the nature of life on earth, the facts tell us of an evolving humanity, a directionality of growth and improvement. Our practice of gratitude helps us see this both personally and collectively. We can begin to believe and feel that all is well.

As our insight into our true nature deepens, from both subjective contemplative and scientific perspectives, we can see that bringing our body, our heart, our mind, our very being into this state of peace and love is a great contribution to the continuation of humanity evolving into higher states of consciousness and functioning. We have touched on how gratitude is a practice and path toward creating this state of consciousness.

In the next chapters, we will look in more detail about how we are one interconnected, immaterial being and the miraculous nature of gratitude. We will come to see how being grateful is not only enjoyable and beneficial for our personal experience but a gift to the world.

Thank you.

PART 4

Gratitude Reveals Truths of Existence

Chapter 11

Unitive Being:
One Undivided Reality

My meditation practice began with a free Sri Chinmoy class after seeing a flyer at a bookstore in Hamilton, New Zealand. This was in the pre-app world! I utilized further instruction from a book, helpfully titled *Meditation,* by another Indian spiritual teacher, Eknath Easwaran. After an intriguing first session in which I sensed the benefits such practice can deliver, I began to meditate on my own with the help of this book.

Like many people who sit down to meditate for the first time, one of the first insights gained was the busy nature of the thinking mind and how it was happening beyond my control. In my years of sharing meditation with people, I have realized that sadly, many people are put off by encountering this initial insight. Believing mediation to be an absence of thought, they perceive fault in the busy mind they encounter, conclude they cannot meditate, and cease the practice before it has truly begun. Easwaran recognized this as being especially problematic for the often highly stressed Western mind. To counter this issue, he recommended that on beginning to practice, you start with a prayer, poem, or other meaningful spiritual text to act as the object of concentration. Repeating a passage slowly and silently for the duration of the meditation period can serve much like giving an excited dog a bone. Giving the mind something to chew and focus on helps it be calm and focused.

I recall being unsure what text I would choose. There were some poems that came to mind, yet I had an aversion to religion. This aversion came about following my own inquiry into the primary religion of my culture, Christianity. The stories did not make sense, and though many principles resonated as true, the embodiment of these truths appeared lacking. So it is perhaps surprising that I selected the prayer of St. Francis to be the object of my meditation. Perhaps it was hearing that St. Francis had been a bit of a party animal, enjoying wine and women in his early life, that I identified with and found hope within. Or it may simply have been the potent beauty and sense of alchemy the prayer described. I knew I was in need of some alchemy and felt this being spoken to in the prayer.

I encountered a few versions and ended up practicing this one:

Lord, make me an instrument of thy peace

Where there is hatred, let me sow love

Where there is injury, pardon

Where there is doubt, faith

Where there is division, unity

Where there is discord, harmony

Where there is despair, hope

Where there is darkness, light

Where there is sadness, joy

O Divine Master, grant that I may not so much seek
  to be consoled as to console

To be understood as to understand

To be loved as to love

For it is in giving that we receive

It is in pardoning that we are pardoned

And it is in dying *to self* that we are born to eternal
  life

I have highlighted two words that are not in every version. To this day, I am unsure where I encountered the subtly yet profoundly different words. I feel that these words transform the prayer from an expression of standard church doctrine—worship of Jesus such that when the body dies, we go to heaven—to a more true teaching of what Jesus, St. Francis, and many other teachers from many different traditions have taught: that heaven is a state of consciousness that can be experienced while alive in this body and that heaven or eternal life is the experience of selflessness, the experience of the cessation of the time-based, self-referencing thought system we call me. Though these days much meditation is practiced to improve health, reduce stress, or become more efficient at work, this is the deeper function of any concentration practice. Whether Zazen, centering prayer, or Vipassana, they all have the potential to allow the "death" of self. In neuroscientific terms, this is speculated to involve the deactivating of the default-mode network and an activating of different parts of the brain.

In addition to such practice, and the tried and tested path of service—putting others before our self—I have found radical gratitude to be an effective means of facilitating this experience of the self-activity ceasing. Let me explain. In chapters 5 and 8, we looked at how the self forms in relationship with something, whether a person, sight, sound, or feeling. A depressed state arises, and thought says, "I am depressed." We experience love when in the presence of another, and thought says, "I love you." In each instance, the movement of the mind is either toward or away from. In Buddhist terms, we would speak of desire or aversion, or in another way of describing the same phenomena, we might say the mind is seeking pleasure or fearing pain. We have looked at how resistance to what is, is the very essence of the suffering self. We can see from this how surrendering to what is, or dying to self, is the end of suffering.

In practical terms, this is simply saying thank you to that which we were resisting. Whether emotional pain, a driver we react to, or someone who appears to insult us, a simple thank-you entirely reframes and transforms the experience. This is the alchemy of gratitude and the realization of the infinite and eternal being, the eternal life, that you are. We can see easily enough that time and space are phenomena arising in that which we are. We are being.

I repeated the St. Francis prayer thousands of times. Often outside of meditation, I would wonder what "Lord" or "Divine Master" meant for someone of no religious faith and why on earth I was so sincerely repeating this prayer if I did not know what it meant! This lack of mental understanding did not seem to impair the power of the prayer. After thousands of hours meditating on these words, I developed the capacity of concentration such that I could move into eyes-open Zazen meditation. In addition, by my own and others' experience of me, I experienced a whole lot more peace, joy, and love where once there was agitation, despair, and fear.

Affirmation: "I am being here now."

You may have read *Be Here Now*, the spiritual classic by Ram Dass. I recall fondly at a Meeting in Love, Truth and Laughter that I led, a gentleman shared that he had read this book around the time of its original publication yet realized only many years later that it could actually apply to him. He had made the common mistake of believing that lofty spiritual realization is for others. Yet Ram Dass, the Buddha, and Jesus actually point us to our Buddha-nature, our Christ self, our capacity to be here now—our infinite and eternal being.

Repeat these words to yourself slowly and deliberately: *I am being here now.* Allow the mind to become absorbed in the words and the feeling they generate. Play with saying this affirmation out loud, quietly to yourself, and maybe even singing it as you go for a run or a walk in nature.

Notice how this is true: You are being. *I am being here now.* Allow the thoughts to dissolve in the already-here experience of being here now.

Explore how you relate to other people, trees, flowers, and birds when in this state of consciousness. Notice how this state of consciousness is your natural state. Reflect on how gratitude, both radical and "garden variety," and meditation can bring you back to this state that you already are.

Meditation: Realizing You Are Everywhere

Prepare for this awareness exercise with a simple meditation. You can download the audio track for it at http://www.newharb inger.com/42020.

Find a quiet spot where you will not be disturbed.

Bring awareness into the body, noticing sensations, aches, and pains without becoming singularly focused on any one sensation.

Take a deep breath or a few.

For a few minutes, simply breathe and bring awareness to each breath.

After a few minutes, open your eyes if they have been closed.

Look to the upper corner of the room, where the ceiling and walls meet.

Imagine you were there looking down upon you sitting in your meditation pose.

What do you see?

Gently play, curiously, with seeing what you look like from the corner of the room.

Give yourself a few minutes to play with this, to see what you see.

As the image forms, continue to play, and take your consciousness to another location, perhaps outside of your room, house, or even beyond the planet. Again, see how your body is from these different points in time and space.

Like any practice, this may take time to perfect.

You may have found this easy to do if you have done similar exercises before and have a natural aptitude. Just as some people pick up a musical instrument and almost immediately make something that sounds like music, you may have a natural gift for expanding and playing with your consciousness. Personally, music is not one of my strongest intelligences, though I have been able to learn and develop (very) basic capacities. It is simply a matter of willingness, desire, and application. I discovered this on a qigong retreat. I had believed myself to be "not a very visual person" and thus doubted my capacity to visualize my brain. When I tried, I failed and could see nothing of my body's inner workings, much as you may have failed to transport your consciousness on your first attempts. After persisting, in a moment of sudden clarity, I could see my brain, blood vessels, cerebrospinal fluid, and all sorts of detail, as if I had X-ray vision. I realized that my consciousness is nonlocal, occurring everywhere. The above meditation has the potential to give you a similar direct experience of unitive being or consciousness. Even if you are not immediately able to experience this directly and are not feeling sufficient curiosity or willingness to practice, you can also consider the fact that many people can have such unitive experiences. Remote viewing, telepathy, clairaudience, and clairsentience are four examples of parapsychological phenomena for which there is, to say it conservatively, data anomalistic to the predominant metaphysics of physicists that is reductive materialism. Reductive materialism is the idea that reality is fundamentally made of matter, of particles, and that analysis of all parts of the whole will reveal the whole's workings, much as what analyzing the cogs and wheels of a clock would do. This belief affirms that all happenings of mind including consciousness itself are consequences of, or caused by, matter. Yet the capacity to experience consciousness in a place where your brain is not, or even when the brain has died as we saw in chapter 8, brings this belief into question via direct experience.

Separation is an illusion, a creation of our brain. It certainly seems like there is an "out there" and "in here," a world of separate objects, including me, yet on closer examination, we see this is not true. We can perceive oneness when we recognize the essence and presence of our own being, and then notice it in the trees, birds, flowers, even the concrete. It is experienced not only by our own direct experience but by the most repeated, verified, peer-reviewed science known to humanity: the science of the quantum.

Quantum Mechanics

The brilliance of science as a system of discovering and stating truth is its ability to correct and revise itself. Most belief systems are unwilling to recognize the beliefs of other wisdom traditions or indeed any evidence that runs counter to their beliefs. The Dalai Lama is an exception among religious leaders when he invites scientists to test the assertions of his faith. In stating, "If scientific analysis were conclusively to demonstrate certain claims in Buddhism to be false, then we must accept the findings of science and abandon those claims" (Dalai Lama 2006, 3), he aligns himself with the true skeptic by exhibiting the open heart and mind essential for any scientist who wishes to stay true to science.

This open-mindedness was put to the test like never before when in 1900 Max Planck determined that light was made of individual units, or quanta. Then in 1905, Einstein theorized that energy and radiation were similarly made of quanta. In 1925, quantum mechanics was truly born, with Heisenberg, Born, Jordan, Schrödinger, Jeans, de Broglie, and Pauli as the key players in the creation of a science that has turned the predominant worldview upside down. So completely has quantum mechanics challenged our view of how reality works that we are still searching for a unified theory that integrates classical Newtonian mechanics—the good stuff that has us flying in airplanes in a safe and predictable fashion—with quantum mechanics.

To be clear, I am not a physicist of any ilk. This might be an advantage, though, as it means I can come to research with slightly fresher eyes than those who have been conditioned through many years of academia. Curiously, one of the most striking aspects of this field is a lack of agreement as to what quantum mechanics really is or is saying. Indeed, what is agreed upon is that no one really understands it. There is agreement among many leading lights of the field that its incomprehensibility is an essential aspect. I suggest this incomprehensibility is largely a consequence of how quantum physics undermines or clashes with our preexisting ideas of time, space, matter, energy, linearity, and causality. Perhaps most crucially and unspeakably profoundly, it demonstrates consciousness to be primary and causative. In proving that matter is not truly a thing, not solid matter, but is probability, simultaneously wave and particle, and affected by the content or intention of the observing consciousness, quantum mechanics is insisting we develop a worldview that incorporates these findings. It is a worldview totally different from how we were brought up and how our experience of ordinary consciousness perceives reality. In my view, quantum mechanics is telling us that reality only becomes reality in the observing of it in consciousness. This is a view shared by the late Nobel prize–winning Hungarian American theoretical physicist, mathematician, and engineer Eugene Wigner, at least early on in his career, among other great minds such as John von Neumann. Put very simply, quantum mechanics demonstrates one unitive immaterial-material being. Or as current leading light of the field Henry Stapp puts it, in a more measured and decidedly scientific fashion:

> From the point of view of the mathematics of quantum theory it makes no sense to treat a measuring device as intrinsically different from the collection of atomic constituents that make it up. A device is just another part of the physical universe… Moreover, the conscious thoughts of a human observer ought to be causally connected *most directly and immediately* to what is happening in his brain, not to what is happening out at some measuring device… Our bodies and brains thus become…parts of the quantum mechanically described physical universe. Treating

the entire physical universe in this unified way provides a conceptually simple and logically coherent theoretical foundation. (Stapp 2001)

There is no separation. It is easy to see the problems of such a view that naturally follow. Every concept and each idea with which humanity has mapped and made sense of our experience is up for review. Our interest here, of course, is how a unified view relates to gratitude when we regard our consciousness as a participating factor in the manifestation of the physical world. Clearly a grateful consciousness, seeing the world as good and emphasizing the positive, is desirable. In giving attention to the good, we experience it more.

If the glass is neither half full nor half empty but however you perceive it to be, then how you perceive your "reality" is not a *description* of but a *creation* of reality. Thus, in feeling, seeing, thinking, and *being* grateful, we are creating a world which we can be grateful for. In this view we are aligning with the very beingness of the universe itself, grateful for itself. Phew! Let's now try a more immediate and less mind-boggling way to come into contact with the unitive nature of being and one undivided reality.

Exercise: A Grateful Meal

You have likely heard the idea of saying grace for a meal, of giving thanks. This is a beautiful ritual, and in this practice, we are going to go a step further, expanding our awareness intentionally to see the true nature of the meal on our plate.

The following exercise can be applied to any meal. The first time you do it, it might be ideal if you are alone to allow you to be undistracted and take the exercise to its fullest realization. The steps below are by no means prescriptive but a guide. Let your mind flow with the appreciation and expand in gratitude.

In the instructions below, I use an omnivore's meal. Of course, the same can be applied to a vegan or vegetarian meal.

> Looking at the plate and the food on the plate, the table, knife, and fork, take in the whole scene, aware of each constituent part.

> Observe and feel appreciation for the plate and the person who first invented the plate, ceramics, and the person who designed, produced, and brought this plate to the store from where you purchased it.

> Repeat this process with the knife, fork, and table. Contemplate the people who would have to have been involved in inventing, designing, and creating these items, in the first instance and for this specific item you are utilizing.

> If you are at a wooden table, feel gratitude and give thanks for the tree, the wood, the lumberjack, the saw, the saw's inventor, the department store.

Assuming your cutlery is stainless steel, give thanks and feel gratitude for the creation of such an alloy, for the chrome, nickel, and steel, for the first human to discover metals upon the earth, for the first human to discover fire and begin to experiment with the creation of such tools.

Now come to the food! Observe the vegetables and give and feel thanks for their beauty and the nutrients they will bring into your body. Feel appreciation for the sun, earth, and water that co-created this food item for you.

Bring gratitude to the person who harvested the crop, the driver who transported it to the market or shop, the shelf-stacker, the cashier, the CEO of the supermarket.

Repeat this with each vegetable or salad item, connecting with the life force of the vibrant plant, root, or fruit that is now available to boost your own.

For the meat, fish, or other protein source, give especially reverent thanks and appreciation. If it's animal protein, connect with the spirit of that animal that has given its life force to support your own.

Feel gratitude for the life force that each item contains which is soon to be absorbed into your blood.

Eat each mouthful mindfully, giving thanks for your teeth, digestive system, saliva, and sense of taste. Imagine the nutrients and goodness, energy, and well-being absorbed into every corner of your body.

Enjoy the tastes and give thanks to the whole world, planet earth, the sun, and the history of humanity that has conspired to bring you this meal!

On completing this meal, reflect on how the history of humanity, an army of millions, was required to bring this food to your plate. Reflect on how viewing the meal this way altered your experience of eating this meal.

Of course, the above is not practical or necessary every time you eat a meal. However, using gratitude to clearly see the fullness of any meal set before you will allow you to tap into the same appreciation and gratitude in future meals in a moment of reflection.

To truly maximize the impact of this exercise, share it with your family or friends who are open. Adjust it to a length and format that works for you and guide the experience of opening to the true beauty, the vast net of human creativity, ingenuity, and work; the powerful interplay of the sun, earth, and water that is essential to every meal we will ever eat.

Imagine if each meal became a signifier, a symbol, and a reminder of the interconnected web of life that is always loving and caring for us so generously.

Gratefully Living the Paradox

In exploring unitive being, one undivided reality, we have encountered several paradoxes central to human experience.

On the one hand, I am an individuated being with a unique flavor of personality, collection of personas, sub-personalities, and so forth. I am unique just like everyone else. At the same time I am being, unitive, one with all else. I am simultaneously water drop, fluid and ever changing; snowflake, the particular expression of beauty, my fingerprint or divine blueprint; and ocean, the vast conscious presence permeating all phenomena.

On the one hand, I am perfect as I am, in beingness, the ocean. At the same time I am becoming more, a fluid and ever-changing water drop and more and more an expression of the uniqueness of my essence, the snowflake.

The prayer of St. Francis speaks powerfully to this becoming more of the peaceful, joyful, loving being I am.

The practice of radical gratitude, saying thank you to all phenomena, experience, and challenge, is a recognition of our always becoming. It is an honoring of the perpetual opportunity for the death and rebirth of self. In the releasing of resistance, suffering ceases. Here we are able to taste the alchemical power of thank you. To share again that quote attributed to Wayne Dyer and Max Planck, a founding father of quantum mechanics and appreciator of the *Tao Te Ching,* "When we change the way we look at things, the things we look at change."

In thank you, we are in union with Life or "God," if you prefer. In thank you, we are in peace and joy; we are in unitive being.

The practice of playing with our consciousness to perceive from other points in time-space our body is inhabiting gives us the direct experience of oneness, everywhere, yet simultaneously here now and individuated.

The affirmation *I am being here now* is a reminder for the mental body of what is deeper than and beyond the mental body. It reminds us of and evokes the felt knowing of being.

The messy mystery of quantum mechanics—a sort of modern mysticism, a revelation of the nature of consciousness to the nature of consciousness by the nature of consciousness—gives us a groundless grounding for the craziness and paradoxes of experience. Our dualistic minds, so conditioned to think in terms of left and right, right and wrong, dark and light, in the West especially, can literally not grasp, perceive, or express the nondual. Our yin and yang symbols are rather more hidden away in esotericism. Yet in quantum physics, we have an inexplicable explanation of the inexplicable. We discover that, like it or not, reality is wave and particle simultaneously. We realize that we are conscious participants in the determination of one or the other. We are creating in our observing. And through this lens, we see the truth and the true power of gratitude: the creation here and now of the reality of "heaven on earth," the experience of unified being. From this perspective, we can see how our being grateful is a most beneficial collapsing of the wave function, a genuine contribution to our well-being and the well-being of all. In the coming chapter, we will see how our practicing gratitude is a gift for all and how it is true not only that in giving we receive, but also that in receiving we give.

Thank you.

Chapter 12

Your All-Inclusive Effort Uplifts the World

When I was diagnosed with brain cancer, I was advised to "get my affairs in order." Having a very simple financial life and no dependents meant this was relatively straightforward when it came to my financial affairs. I advised the lawyer simply, "Half to Mum, half to Dad, and any debts belong to no one!"

However, I felt a deeper meaning in this instruction, beyond financial affairs: to ensure that everything that needed to be said was completed while I could. With my family, this led to one memorable afternoon sitting outside in the summer sunshine on my mother's patio. My parents' divorce had been a hugely difficult time for us all. I was aware that it was likely still the case that someone felt regret or guilt around what happened. I wanted to do all I could to ensure no such wastage of energy or unnecessary suffering occurred in relation to my own illness. So, I spoke to my family as one and communicated three things as clearly and powerfully as I knew how. The first was that no one need feel any guilt, shame, or regret for what happened, at any point in our family's life. I explained how I saw and experienced all the difficulty, that it was all perfect, all opportunity for growth and learning, and could not have been other than it was. Second, I expressed the depth and totality of my love for each member of my family. And third, I expressed the sincerest thanks to my mother, father, and sister, for being all they had been, doing all they had done, and playing such wonderful roles in my life. You can perhaps imagine the profundity, the poignancy, the bittersweetness of this occasion and how ultimately uplifting this would be for Mum, Dad, and Louise, my relationship with each, and the family dynamic.

I share the above because it illustrates in one example what I have observed in many others—that my transformation, clarity, and well-being impact my family. In turn, the effects upon my family will ripple out into their relationships and into the community, then into our society, nation, and planetary community. This story gives an indication of how our personal transformation has immediately observable ripples and effects upon the world around us. There are many more unseen effects too.

From a belief system built on the foundations of separation and materialism, many further falsehoods flow. These include the ideas that to help others, I need to help others, that when I help myself I am only helping myself, and that within a physical world of separate being, my personal work can benefit only me. Thus, I forged a career in charity fundraising believing that helping others was the greatest gift I could bring to the world.

We have erroneously believed in such ideas as that separation exists and that we are primarily physical beings living in a primary physical world where only linear cause and effect is in operation.

Yet we have come to know there is no such thing as separation. It is an "optical delusion of consciousness," to use Einstein's words from a letter he wrote to Dr. Robert Marcus in 1950. We are coming to see we are immaterial conscious beings living in an immaterial conscious universe.

Wolfgang Pauli and Carl Jung coined the term "synchronicity," an acausal connecting principle that is a complementary way that reality unfolds (Jung 1960). Just as Newtonian mechanics is linear and predictable and offers cause and effect, quantum mechanics is nonlinear and allows for unpredictable novelty. This dichotomy gives us synchronicity. Cause and effect and synchronicity are two simultaneously true, mutually complementary lenses with which to understand, navigate, and create reality.

A critical aspect of synchronistic phenomena, and a way that the individual consciousness has the direct experience of oneness, is that the meaning of two events coinciding is found in the subjectivity of the observer. There is no causal connection but rather a connection that is known through the consciousness observing. In seeing again and again how "outer" and "inner" interact, we lose the need for such conceptual distinctions. We gain the clarity that the universe's evolution and expansion are achieved via our individuated expansion and evolution.

It was through synchronicity that I was led to be in the presence of Zen master Jun Po Denis Kelly Roshi and experience a transformation from suffering self to awakened being, within seconds of being in his presence—a glimpse or "Keisho" to cultivate into full awakening or "Satori." This demonstrated to me the communication that our being, our state of consciousness, is always having with the world around us. It made clear in my mind that Gandhi was offering a profound truth in the idea, "Be the change we want to see in the world." When we are in a state of inner peace, love, and joy, we create a more peaceful, loving, and joyful world. When we feel grateful, the world feels more grateful. Our actions and attempts to improve the world will be that much more powerful and sustainable when coming from this place of overflow.

A simple example illustrates how we must first help ourselves to be able to truly help others. On an airplane, you have likely heard the advice to, in the event of an emergency, put an oxygen mask on yourself before your child. It is easy to see why. We take the action we can take, while we can take the action, in order to remain able to help another. Our cultivating a state of gratitude, of feeling good, of well-being can be regarded as consciously connecting to the flow of love, of life force, such that we are well resourced, overflowing, in order to then most impactfully help others.

Affirmation: *"In giving, I am receiving, and in receiving, I am giving."*

The first half of this line in St. Francis's prayer is a necessary pointer to the reality that in contributing to the whole, in giving, we feel good. Truly, in giving, we receive.

In working with groups in support of healing, transformation, and awakening, I have found that often we are very well practiced at giving. Our kindness, our desire to help and to ensure others' well-being, is fairly well established. Instead, it is in truly *receiving* love, kindness, compliments, attention, help, money, or other things where we may need a little practice, an invitation to receive. This can be aided by recognizing that in receiving we facilitate giving—just as we might need to learn to give so we might need to learn to receive. The two are of course mutually dependent. Gratitude is a way of consciously and graciously giving thanks *and* receiving.

A coaching client recently explained that she felt guilty feeling such joy and well-being in her new love affair because a fellow member of our group was experiencing the challenge and difficulty of a divorce. This person is a mother, and I find this attitude especially strong in mothers in general. It seems that many have so successfully and wholly embodied the selfless role of being a parent that it is necessary to then practice being willing to open and receive love and care from others. There is a transition from being primarily responsible for others' well-being to being primarily responsible for one's own well-being. Of course, anyone who has ever been mothered by someone depleted in their own well-being knows how valuable it is for a parent to be resourced in their own peace and joy.

There is a wider societal issue at play in the Western world, it seems. This is well illustrated by the story of Sharon Salzberg in conversation with the Dalai Lama decades ago. Now a well-established and highly respected spiritual teacher in the US, a young Salzberg is reported to have responded to the Dalai Lama's talk on cultivating compassion for others with a question on what meditations might exist to cultivate compassion for oneself. This perplexed the Dalai Lama, as the compassion meditations automatically include the person meditating. The issue of self-esteem or guilt was simply not an issue in Tibetan culture—perhaps because their culture is absent of religions and marketing that try to convince people that they are guilty or lacking in order to sell their religion or face cream! The term "self-compassion" came into use to emphasize this need to bring kindness and care to ourselves as well as others.

Now of course, when I am able to receive your kindness or compliment or assistance, you are given the joy of giving, the contentment of having helped another, of having made a difference. In receiving, I allow the love to flow through you without impediment. A helpful reframe perhaps to keep in mind is that giving and receiving are two aspects of the same movement, and we need to learn both.

Try saying, "In giving, I am receiving, and in receiving, I am giving." How does it feel? Experiment by repeating this to yourself silently, out loud, or if you feel called, sing it! If you are a mother transitioning as your children leave home and become self-reliant, this may well be your anthem for this time.

We need no excuse or justification to feel good, be happy, or live in joy. Well-being is its own reward, for ourselves and all with whom we come into contact. When we have mastered self-sourcing our own well-being, we may then find ourselves helping others to accomplish the very same. At the same time we can each accomplish this only for ourselves. And gratitude, for giving and receiving, is key to this.

Meditation: Being Love Loving

Find a quiet spot where you will not be disturbed, sit in a comfortable posture that you can maintain for twenty minutes, and set your meditation timer. Download the audio for this meditation at http://www.newharbinger.com/42020.

Take a few deep breaths in your own time.

Bring awareness to where your body, ankles, buttocks, knees, or the soles of your feet are in contact with the floor.

Notice how you are held to the ground, how gravity and the earth hold you.

Complete a brief free-flowing body scan for a few moments. Allow attention to move by itself to tension, ache, sensation, and on to the next.

Become aware of breath, whether the rise and fall of the chest or the movement of air on the lips, through the nostrils, or atop the upper lip. Simply notice a few breaths, changing nothing, just observing how it is.

Allow awareness to drop into the center of your chest, the heart center.

Begin to breathe in and out of your heart center, as if you had a mouth or a nose in your chest.

On the in-breath, inhale love, whether as a color, pink, green, or golden white; the word; or the feeling.

On the out-breath, perceive the beautiful globe, Mother Earth, full of the billions of our brothers and sisters, and breathe this love such that it enters and surrounds the earth.

Continue to breathe in love and breathe out love into and around the earth such that you see it begin to glow more and more.

Enjoy the symbiosis as breathing in and out more love creates a visually more loved and loving globe.

Continue enjoying until the timer sounds. (Or keep going if you wish!)

Sit with the feelings and the afterglow for a little while. How is it to experience directly that your well-being, your being loved, and the well-being of others and of the planet are one and the same? As with all the meditations in this book, consider doing this as a mini-meditation that you utilize or offer as you are going about your day. Public transit is a great place to play with this. Rather than the whole globe, see the loving energy envelop, surround, and penetrate the train, bus, or plane. Once again in such situations, notice how your giving and receiving are one flow of loving presence that you are.

Global Coherence and Intergenerational Trauma

Though the astrology in your tabloid newspaper may indeed be lacking much substance, you may be surprised to hear that the correlations between planetary activity and human behavior, and between the individual and collective, are actually well documented. Not only that, but trauma you experience now may show up (or perhaps not if you are able to heal and integrate it) in the experience of your grandchildren.

The science of interconnectedness is in its infancy. As we have seen in the last chapter, the data of quantum mechanics pose significant challenges to our most fundamental assumptions about how the world works and thus how and what to scientifically study. Similarly, chaos theory has begun to ripple out into our thinking. You have surely heard of the butterfly effect. Here, the example is of a butterfly flapping its wings on one side of the world leading to a hurricane on the other. The example is used to illustrate the idea of how one small change in a state of a nonlinear deterministic system can have large effects on a later state. As quantum mechanics makes clear, reality is a nonlinear (non)deterministic system. Within this system, a subtle adjustment here or there, whether within your consciousness or in the sun's solar flare activity, can lead to massive effects in the future.

Richard Tarnas's book *Cosmos and Psyche* (2006) is a helpful introduction to the surprising and remarkable correlation between planetary movements and human affairs, including revolutions and the like.

Meanwhile the Global Coherence Initiative (GCI) is one organization applying a scientific lens to the effects of changes in the earth's magnetic field. Their studies explore correlations between solar flare activity and significant global events with measures such as violent crime, social unrest, and admissions to hospital emergency departments. The working hypotheses of the GCI include:

1. Human and animal health, cognitive function, emotions, and behavior are affected by solar, geomagnetic, and other earth-related magnetic fields.

2. The earth's magnetic field is a carrier of biologically relevant information that connects all living systems.

3. Every person affects the global information field.

4. Collective human consciousness affects the global information field. Therefore, large numbers of people creating heart-centered states of care, love, and compassion will generate a more coherent field environment that can benefit others and help offset the current planetary discord and incoherence. (HeartMath Institute, 2018)

A growing network of sites monitoring the earth's magnetic field and evolving technology measuring the coherence of the individual human heart and other aspects of the autonomic nervous system are key in this fascinating area of scientific inquiry.

As the GCI website states:

The GCMS [Global Coherence Monitoring System] sensors continuously monitor the resonant frequencies in Earth's magnetic field. They track changes in geomagnetic activity caused by solar storms, changes in solar wind speed, disruption of the Schumann resonances (SR) and, potentially, the signatures of major global events that have a strong emotional component.

It is well established that the resonant frequencies in the earth's various magnetic fields directly overlap with those of the human brain, cardiovascular and autonomic nervous systems. Therefore, it should not be surprising that numerous physiological rhythms in humans and global collective behaviors are not only synchronized with solar and geomagnetic activity, but that disruptions in these fields can create adverse effects on human health and behavior. When the earth's magnetic field environment is disturbed it can cause sleep disturbance, mental confusion, unusual lack of energy or a feeling of being on edge or overwhelmed for no apparent reason. (HeartMath Institute, 2018)

Meanwhile, as mentioned earlier in the book, researchers such as Rachel Yehuda have discovered evidence appearing to support the idea of intergenerational trauma. If it is possible for trauma to be inherited, it seems reasonable to conclude that our efforts to heal and integrate trauma may also yield inherited effects.

These two areas of study offer intriguing support for the idea that an individual's present state of physiology and psychology are both effects and causes of current collective and future individual experience. Within one unitive immaterial being, there really is no such thing as separate personal experience! Coupled with many other areas of research, we begin to see a new paradigm emerge that accounts for all the data, both classical and quantum, while profoundly empowering the human being. We are beginning to map possible mechanisms for how practicing gratitude now, as an integral part of our efforts to self-resource love and well-being, can have benefits far beyond our own experience and even our own life.

Exercise: My Well-Being Serves Humanity

We have begun to see how our personal well-being and that of others are interrelated and even that to help ourselves is to help others. Let's take this a step further and create more clarity in our thinking of how our personal happiness, health, and prosperity help us help others and benefit the world.

For this exercise you will need pen and paper.

Begin writing at the top of a page: *When I am over-flowing with more than enough well-being, vibrant health, and money, I better serve the world by…*

On each line beneath, add a benefit.

For example, I might write *being able to offer a smile and kindness to strangers*, or more generally *being a source of well-being for all who encounter me.*

With respect to health, I might write *having the energy, vibrancy, and fitness to volunteer.*

Or with respect to having more than enough money, I may reflect: *being able to give freely to homeless people or to charities I care about or to assist friends and family, being able to buy organic food and earth-friendly products and carbon-offsetting flights, being able to give more time to meditation and going on retreat or funding others to do the same.*

Hopefully it is clear that your abundance in peace and joy, your inner well-being, and physical and financial health, your outer well-being, is a first step toward being able to be a greater positive impact upon others and the world as a whole. How does this insight affect how you might think about and prioritize your own well-being?

Becoming Servants of Humanity Via Our Well-Being

The desire to help, to contribute to better a world of much suffering, challenge, and difficulty, is entirely natural. We can see clearly too that we are a part of this world and that culturally we are sometimes blind to this—giving compassion yet somehow forgetting to include and nourish our own compassionate being.

In exploring the interconnected nature of existence, we can begin to see that personal development work, spiritual practice, personal healing, and time nourishing our own well-being are far from selfish. Instead, we can recognize that self-love and self-care are both a foundation of our being of service in the world and in and of themselves beneficial to others. Just as we are advised on airplanes to affix our own mask before helping others, we may recognize that becoming well sourced in our well-being is a necessary foundation for our taking action to help others or heal the planet.

In looking at some of the ways that separate physical beings affect other physical beings, both alive now and passed or yet to be born, we open up a new view of interconnectedness and thus the impact of our state of consciousness. We are all connected to the same fields of earth's magnetism and to our ancestors and descendants via our genetics, which are affected by our current and consistently held state of consciousness.

In our meditation and exercise, we may see the correlation and indeed the oneness of our feeling good and the world being loved and healed, the simultaneity of our abundance and the abundance of other beings. We can make the powerful distinction that unlike some resources, money is an infinite resource, like our universe ever expanding, and that in our receiving more of this resource, others also receive more. We can see this wonderful paradox unified: in giving, we receive, and in receiving, we give.

Within all this, we begin to deepen our reverence and appreciation for this gratitude, this gratefulness, as being the essential energy or vibration at the core of this eternal interplay. We may feel gratitude for gratitude itself. Indeed, we may come to see gratitude as being the essence of, pointing to, and giving the direct experience of one other eternal truth, the truth of love.

Thank you.

Chapter 13

Love Is the Only Truth

Many years ago, I watched a movie called *Love Actually* in which the narrator begins by saying something like, "When I look around me, all I see is love." I recall experiencing an extraordinarily self-righteous angry reaction. It went something like, *Of course you do—you are a millionaire in Islington. If only you saw the real world.* My reaction came back to me when reflecting on a key aspect of my healing journey: the depth of transformation gratitude has facilitated and a truth of existence that gratitude reveals. I have realized that love is indeed everywhere and that our perceiving it depends not on where we live or how much money we have, but on our willingness to be fully awake as consciousness and open to receiving.

In this closing chapter, we are going to explore and experience gratitude as a means to fully awaken, to open to receive and realize the presence of love. Gratitude can help us realize love is indeed everywhere. As we have seen, our capacity to perceive love and to see love in the eyes of another who may be experiencing fear is transformational not just for ourselves but for the world as a whole. If "gratitude is heaven," as William Blake put it (1906), then our being immersed in gratitude means taking heaven wherever we go, being a beacon of love in a fearful world.

In chapter 4, I touched on how in my healing journey, I naturally explored all avenues to health. I was guided in synchronistic fashion to a healer who had cured his cancer and helped others heal their own brain tumors, among other ailments. It was the late Martin Brofman, author of *Anything Can Be Healed*, who advised that the psychospiritual aspect of any brain condition was an acute tension in consciousness associated with issues with authority, physical father, and "the Father"—our relationship with the divine, however we conceive or do not conceive of it.

The psychospiritual aspect of a brain condition is but one aspect among many. But what Martin was saying made total sense to me and felt like a helpful line of inquiry. I had prayed to God, as I conceived of It, to not let my parents get divorced when I was in my early teens and their marriage was unraveling. My upbringing was not very religious—we sang hymns at school, and as a family would attend church at Easter or Christmas, but this was perhaps more a social function than deep faith. I was very much trying to work out whether Christianity or atheistic reductive materialism were true. Looking back, praying to God was a sort of experiment in this inquiry. In my immaturity, I petitioned and attempted to convince God that my parents' staying together was best for all: for my family, the village, and society as a whole. "Not for me, God, but for so many others" was my rationale. So, if God was good, existed, and cared, then surely God would grant this wish! If life was good and cared, it would surely look like a happy, longer-lasting marriage! The fury I felt at life and at my parents over my perception of their role in affairs was huge. This anger and resentment I held projected out to society as a whole, to politicians, teachers, and business leaders for being so ignorant, hypocritical, and causing so much utterly avoidable injustice and suffering. I held a lot of anger in my body and felt fearful, in an unsafe world.

On a healing retreat with Martin, I discovered that I rather clashed with this authority figure, though I was able to remain sufficiently humble and open to receive an extraordinary gift. He looked me in the eyes and said with conviction, as if offering a definitive diagnosis, "You just need to open to the love of your father." As he said this, a deep coil of energy in my body and emotional system began to unravel. Tears began to gently stream down my face, and I sensed a huge outburst of pent-up emotion. Perhaps typical of my Englishness, I politely made my excuses and went to my hotel room, where I allowed the most intense release of emotion. My body pulsated and shook as I wailed and sobbed. Tears and snot aplenty were expelled from my system.

At the earliest opportunity, when it became a reasonable hour, I called my father. I simply stated that I had realized I had blocked myself from receiving his love these last twenty years and that I was receiving it now and intended to remain open to receiving it and to create a new, richer, deeper relationship with him. You can perhaps imagine the emotional intensity for both my father and me. We both cried. My father had loved and cared for me wonderfully well all my life and had called me in Australia every day for months following the diagnosis. However, it was only then that I fully opened to feel his love, absorb his love, *receive* his love.

In that moment, as tears rolled down my face, a curious sensation that felt very much like tears running up my temples occurred. Of course, I knew gravity only goes in one direction and was perplexed by this cranial sensation. And I was a little excited—here I was on a healing journey, looking for the psychospiritual key, and in having discovered this possible causative factor in my health, I experienced an immediate and powerful physiological response in the very part of the body where the issue was located. The sensation felt undeniably good. I was delighted and sure that this was a breakthrough, the breakthrough in creating healing and health.

The next day, I had an appointment with another gifted healer, Dan Lappin. Dan was based up the road from the hotel in San Rafael, California, where the healing seminar was being held, in Mill Valley. I had experienced some powerful sessions with Dan previously, including one in which I had released so much anger so loudly, so violently, so powerfully, that he had to go and reassure the hairdressers below that all was well! I felt that my work with Dan was complete, yet something told me to go to the appointment nonetheless. Within minutes of sitting down and without my sharing anything of my experience in the previous twenty-four hours, Dan felt to speak to the hormone production that occurs in each temple. In one, vasopressin is produced. This hormone is particularly prevalent in males and is associated with creating boundaries, protecting a mate, and the like. He went on to explain that the other temple produces oxytocin, also known as the love hormone, especially prevalent in females, and of course, all about love. Here, as so often on the healing journey, I encountered just the right person or piece of information at just the right time.

Again, here, I speak to my own experience. However, it was a powerful one. I felt immense gratitude for this and perceived it to be evidence of a loving universe, a loving world that somehow cared about my well-being and healing. In a similar way, opening our perception to the abundance of loving gifts, such as the multitudinous expressions of beauty upon this exquisite planet, in gratitude, allows us to experience that we are loved. Expanding our gratitude to include the unpleasant phenomena, challenges, and painful emotional or physical experiences and uncovering the gift, opportunity, or learning even allows love to be perceived in our suffering. As we come into appreciative contact with the very essence of our existence, the gifts of breath, being, and awareness open us to a moment-to-moment experience of being loved.

Affirmation: *"I am loved."*

I believe we are all yearning deep down for the experience of feeling love and of feeling loved. We can be like fish looking for water or like a poor man unaware that he has a diamond in his pocket.

Typically we seek love, as the song goes, in all the wrong places. Whether in food, alcohol, sex, work, thought, or romantic partnership, we may explore all outer phenomena until we discover the love within our own heart, the love within each breath.

Repeat this simple phrase and see how easy or difficult it is to allow the mental phrasing to bring you into the felt somatic experience of being loved: *I am loved.*

Play with the breath as carrier of love, with the self-hug exercises, and the accompanying mental reminder. Bring a lightness of heart and a playful spirit to this exercise.

Whatever comes up in your experience, an unworthy thought, a difficult sensation, or a narrative of unlovability, love this too. Be persistent and complete in your willingness to receive love in every aspect of your experience.

If it helps, bring attention to the breath now being given and the awareness and being with which you are now graced, regardless of anything you do or think, to convince the mind to open the heart to the feeling of being loved.

As ever, play with speaking out loud or silently, or singing as you dance around your room.

Meditation: Forgiveness

In this meditation we are going to use the same practice in chapter 12 yet with a profound addition. We are going to receive love into our hearts and into the image of someone who has harmed us or toward whom we hold resentment, however justified the resentment may seem. You can download audio for this practice at http://www.newharbinger.com /42020.

Find a quiet spot where you will not be disturbed, sit in a comfortable posture that you can maintain for twenty minutes, and set your meditation timer. To prepare, invite life, source, spirit, the universe, whatever works for you to help you in the act of forgiveness.

Take a few deep breaths in your own time.

Bring awareness to where your body, ankles, buttocks, knees, or the soles of your feet are in contact with the floor.

Notice how you are held to the ground, how gravity and the earth have you held.

Complete a brief free-flowing body scan for a few moments. Allow attention to move by itself to tension, ache, sensation, and on to the next.

Become aware of breath, whether the rise and fall of the chest or the movement of air on the lips, through the nostrils, or atop the upper lip. Simply notice a few breaths, changing nothing, just observing how it is.

Allow awareness to drop into the center of your chest, the heart center.

Begin to breathe in and out of your heart center, as if you had a mouth or a nose in your chest.

Visualize someone you perceive to have harmed you, someone whom you hold resentment toward. If no one comes to mind, select the first parent or caregiver that comes to mind.

On the in-breath, inhale love, whether as a color, pink, green, or golden white; the word; or the feeling.

On the out-breath, perceive gratitude, feel thanks, whether via the word, the feeling, a color, or another signifier of the experience of gratitude.

Continue to breathe in love and breathe out gratitude such that you feel each more and more deeply toward the person you selected.

Enjoy the experience of breathing as the ongoing recognition of the gift and expression of love that it is.

Continue enjoying until the timer sounds. (Or keep going if you wish.)

Sit with the feelings and enjoy the afterglow for a little while. How is it to allow forgiveness? Reflect on how readily and easily you were able to forgive and whether this may reflect your experience of relating with family members, with lovers, or indeed with a common symbol of life force or love—money. Consider how the energetic stance of being receptive to love, consciously allowing this flow to be enjoyed and appreciated, may be supportive of you more deeply feeling and experiencing love in all aspects of your life.

As with all the meditations in this book, consider incorporating this as a mini-meditation that you utilize as you are going about your day. Whether on your way to work or when you have a quiet moment during the busyness of your day, meditate on the experience of love, of peace, and of easeful joy.

The Power of Love and Its Presence

Studies have shown that a child's development is hugely impacted by the degree to which that child is held and loved in their first months. Science proves that love is essential for the normal development of a human nervous system. Along with water and nutrient-rich food, the human requires love to flourish and be in good health. Though trauma or distant parents may make our challenge greater, as adults, we are able to self-source love. As we have seen in this book, there are many ways we can give ourselves love. The practice of gratitude for our generous and abundant life, self-hugging, mirror work, and the willingness to bring our awareness to all our aches, pains, wounds, and contractions in the physical and emotional body facilitate this. Through the practice of being grateful for our emotions and the unloved parts of ourselves, we come to bring attention and awareness to parts of our experience that we were once unable to. We give ourselves now the loving presence that may have been absent then.

The power of presence, of awareness, and of consciousness itself, as love, can be directly experienced. If we go deep into meditation, here too we may discover that loving is a quality of consciousness itself. Of course, wherever we are, there is consciousness. Wherever we are fully present, there is love.

How does a mother express her love for her child, and how does a partner demonstrate their love for their mate? Through attention, through consciousness.

How does it feel to have someone give you their full and undivided attention? How does it feel to have someone listen, fully, openheartedly, concerned only with your being, your experience, your expression?

We experience attention, openhearted awareness, as loving presence. We can in any moment experience love via our own presence. I can offer two examples where this was put to the test and powerfully demonstrated in my own experience.

Having completed the psychospiritual journey of healing and having opened to love, to life, and on discovering my tumor had not fully resolved itself, I chose to have a conscious craniotomy to remove the tumor. After taking care of the roots, I could now take care of the physical manifestation. I felt immensely grateful that the tumor was operable, thought to be low grade, and that in both Australia and the UK, this operation was available without cost.

I was genuinely excited about the procedure. Having been practicing yoga, qigong, and meditation, I was well prepared to consciously manage my attention and energy through a six-and-a-half-hour experience. I lay on an operating table, in the fetal position, while the surgeon removed pieces of my brain from within my cranium that was bolted to the table. During the procedure, the surgical team would regularly assess my speech and the motor function of my left side to assess whether they could safely continue removing the tumor, or if they might be reaching a point where removing more brain might be too risky. During this, I meditated and directed chi, love, to all parts of my body, my brain especially. There was a memorable moment when I heard the surgeon say to the young doctor in training beside him, "That has higher grade written all over it." I said nothing. I just thought, *Hopefully visual diagnostics is not his strong point!*

The surgery was successfully completed amid much relief with minimal impairment of cognitive or motor function, and the tumor was removed. After the pathology results had come through, the neurosurgical nurse called. She said she would book me in for the neurosurgical clinic next week as had become habit. "By the way," she added, "you will need to book in for the oncology clinic the next day too."

"Oh, that gives me some information!" I replied. It was established that the tumor was categorized as stage 3. It wasn't as bad as some stage 3 tumors, I gratefully noted.

I called my dad and shared the news. "How are you feeling?" my dad asked. I had been feeling disappointment. It was clear I would not be able to fulfill my schedule of talks and events in the next few months as radiotherapy was required. However, on my dad's prompting, I checked in with how I was feeling on a deeper level. I discovered I was feeling joy. On realizing this joy and its juxtaposition with this most interesting development, I felt an immense gratitude. By what grace was there such joy, peace, and love in such a moment!

I continued to cultivate and receive this love and consciously directed it during the radiotherapy treatments too. I utilized cannabis oil and total trust to ensure the treatment was both effective and had the most minimal side effects possible. Now, more than five years from the treatment and seven since diagnosis, I am in perfect health, aware of the presence of love and grateful for it all.

Exercise: All an Expression of, or Invitation for, Love

At the beginning of this book, we looked at the idea that there is always one thing happening, regardless of the shape of our lives or the behavior of others. Here is one helpful possibility for describing this one thing: the movement of love, either expressing itself or inviting itself through its apparent absence. In this world of duality, all exists in opposites where one is necessary for the other. Light depends on darkness, up on down, good on bad, beauty on ugliness, birth on death, love on fear. As a plant seeks light and will move toward it as best as it can, the human seeks love and will move toward it as best as it can.

In this exercise, we are going to discover the transformative power of this perspective in relation to others' behavior (version 1) and our own emotional experience (version 2). You will need pen and paper.

1. Select a person in your life whose behavior troubles you. It could be a president or gang member, a CEO or family member, a greedy capitalist or addicted friend, or an irritating or angry colleague.

Or

2. Select a part of your emotional experience, a recurring contraction in your heart or a persistent shame or sadness.

In each case, open to the full feeling that holding the person or part of you in mind brings up.

Choose to see this person or part of you as a baby, a five-year-old, a ten-year-old, experiencing rejection, abandonment, or trauma.

Recognize this baby or child suffering the withdrawal of love, feeling unloved. Imagine this child growing up and trying to find love through sex, money, power, status, coffee, cocaine.

In the case of your emotional pain, consider that it simply wants your attention and is calling for your unconditional loving presence.

What happens when you see the other or your pain as a hurt child, as a call for love?

Reflect on how helpful this lens might be for supporting your peace of mind and joy. How would your life look if you remembered to first see the innocence of each human, including yourself? How might this be a place of clarity and power from which to act in the world?

Looking Through Love's Eyes

The idea that love is everywhere can seem like an idealistic fantasy, seeing the world through rose-tinted spectacles, out of touch with reality.

Yet we are now aware there is no objective reality, that we are shaping it in how we view things within a participatory universe. We can see that it is possible to move from a fearful, distrusting, lacking view to one that is loving, trusting, and recognizes the abundance of love and good in life and other humans.

Even the most challenging times in life can be experienced to be occurring within the presence of love to the extent we have developed the capacity to be aware of love as a quality of present-moment awareness. We can see that choosing to feel grateful for love is a way to activate a full somatic experience of love.

We have looked at how our capacity to receive love, to see our own innocence, and to see the innocence of another are one and the same and how these are skills that can be learned.

Looking at the idea that everything is either an expression of love or an invitation for love, we have discovered the truth of this, if we are willing to choose to try on these glasses. Perhaps we have tasted how love-tinted glasses are not merely a positive veneer upon reality but actually penetrates into the core of all experience, meeting the inner children within us all seeking love and attention.

The practice of gratitude allows the direct perception of the magnificent abundance of life that we typically take for granted. Opening our perception to the generosity of each present moment, breath by gifted breath, reveals the presence of love.

Thank you.

Conclusion

Throughout this book, we have looked at the power of our choice and how in any moment or circumstance, the meaning we give is causative. The narrative we perceive the world through determines our experience. It is not circumstance that determines our experience but our perception and how consciously and wholeheartedly we are experiencing the moment. Gratitude expands both consciousness and wholeheartedness.

We have realized that the glass of life is neither half full nor half empty but that whatever we decide, we experience the power of our choice and its effect on how we feel. With the knowledge of neurocardiology, we have a story and practices that deepen our capacity to feel grateful for life itself. In accessing intelligence beyond mere thought, we are able to appreciate and experience an integration of head, heart, and gut into a more wholly intelligent human.

Gratitude allows us to be reminded of and see clearly the good of life that we might otherwise overlook. Gratitude helps us see how much life is in fact helping us.

Gratitude is discovered to be a journey into the body and into the pure peace of present-moment awareness. We feel grateful in the body here and now. Indeed, we can feel grateful *for* the body here and now, including its aches, pains, and endlessly changing sensations.

Through the trinity of being, breath, and awareness, we discover an ever-present intertwining of easily touched, unchanging phenomena for which we can feel appreciation.

In looking at our self and our life story through the lens of gratitude, we can come into contact with the beauty and heroism inherent in every human alive. Gratitude for self supports a compassion encompassing all of us.

When the egomind might be running a story of lack and unworthiness, gratitude can allow us to see there is plenty and that we are lovable.

In appreciating the mind as a tool and observing egomind as an innocent puppy rather than a demon, we can begin to create circles of awesomeness rather than viciousness. We can experience the power of gratitude to manage the mind and welcome depression, anxiety, shame, and sadness with a tender appreciative gaze so that we suffer pain less and release trauma more quickly. We can use gratitude to feel more fully so that emotion is less stuck and continues to flow as it naturally does without resistance. In appreciating sadness, despair, and even intense fears and traumas, we can experience the consequence of fully allowing the whole range of human emotion to flow. This consequence is joy. When we are free of resistance to any feeling or emotion, joy flows.

In appreciating awareness itself, we learn we *are* awareness from which ego, egomind, our emotions, thoughts, and the gaps between them are appreciated. In this, we see how gratitude moves us from suffering slave to flourishing master of our experience.

We can step into our creative power as we discover the power of gratitude to create heaven from hell, peace from turbulence, contentment from dissatisfaction, and joy from despair; we can experience the alchemical power of gratitude.

Supported by the knowledge that each such alchemical moment is deepening these grooves of gratitude in our mind and brain, we understand that each effort is investing in capacities of peace, patience, and prosperity to be accessed in times of stress and challenge.

Contemplating how our nervous system is set up to give more of what we feed it, we may feel a great gratitude for this and recognize our awareness of gratitude as such a simple yet powerfully effective stance.

As we familiarize ourselves with generating gratitude in our feeling body, we are discovering an alchemical potion that, when applied liberally to suffering and struggle, can transform them.

In releasing resistance and exercising the muscle of conscious response, whether to bodily sensation, physical circumstance, or the behavior of others, we are accessing universal truths about the nature of existence. In discovering gratitude that is an aspect of awareness itself and a naturally arising element of openhearted awareness, we encounter a universal truth that invites us to meet other universal truths of existence. We may just discover the delicious delight that being, when simply allowed to be, is being grateful. We may laugh as we see gratitude is truly a pathless path, back to itself!

In devotion to gratitude, with patient practice, we can soften the fearful fight-or-flight reactivity to access the knowing and feeling of all being well. Through appreciating our fearful feeling and conditioning for what it is, as it is, and through unconditionally loving presence, we can support our nervous system coming into peace and balance.

In contacting the peace and love of our own innocent being through appreciation, we perceive it in others too.

With the insight, realization, or at least the concept of one unitive being or one consciousness, we begin to grasp the truly miraculous nature of gratitude to transform not only our mind and brain but the world we are co-creating. We observe that in our grateful heart and our overflowing well-being, we are beginning to be truly useful. We can celebrate that in giving, we receive, and in receiving, we give, and we can feel grateful that gratitude is the nexus of this oneness.

Through gratitude, we transform ourselves physically, mentally, emotionally, and spiritually.

A summary on The Greater Good Science Center (n.d.) website reports that hundreds of studies have demonstrated that gratitude can:

- be experienced as one of the most reliable ways of increasing happiness and boosting enthusiasm, optimism, joy, and pleasure

- reduce anxiety and depression

- strengthen the immune system and encourage us to exercise and take good care of our health

- help us sleep better

- increase our resilience and help us recover from trauma more quickly

- promote stronger social bonds, including by encouraging forgiveness

- help children experience greater happiness, resilience, and life satisfaction, and contribute to happier schools.

In transforming ourselves in this way, we in turn naturally affect our families, relationships, communities, and thus the world as a whole. Beyond fleeting time and apparent separation, this grateful heart, this moment imbued with gratitude, ripples into the beyond.

It is my experience that gratitude is to the heart and wellbeing what oxygen is to the lungs and blood. May we breathe in deeply and receive!

Thank you.

Acknowledgments

This book is a culmination of a life's journey and learning. It has been a source of immeasurable joy and gratitude to witness this book take shape through the efforts of an extraordinary team of editors at New Harbinger—thank you Ryan Buresh, Vicraj Gill, Jennifer Holder, Gretel Hakanson, and Melanie Bell. It is no false modesty to state that if the book has a strong structure and reads well, we have these people to thank. For the fact that it has reached you, we can feel gratitude to the expertise and hard work of the marketing team including Julie Bennett, Cassie Kolias, and Analis Souza.

Thank you to my parents and sister Louise for loving me, shaping me, and enduring my teenage self. Thank you to my teachers—those at school who saw something beyond the bluster and posturing, and those in my adult life who have helped me grow up and wake up—Mark Dickinson, Jun Po Denis Kelly Roshi, Doshin Nelson Roshi, Martin Brofman, Mingtong Gu, Alan Seale, Ken Wilber, Tracy Butler, and Dr. Rick Hanson. Gratitude to my friends and associates who have taught by example and in friendship, too numerous to mention but especially Gregor Drugowitsch, Austin Hill Shaw, Ravi Gunaratnam, and Vicky Nicholls. To Henry David Thoreau, Huang Po, Rumi, Hafiz, Jesus Christ, Gautama Buddha, and all whose being has reverberated past their passing into my being now, I bow and say thank you.

I am grateful too for the many people and organizations who have contributed to my growth and well-being and helped me to help others in theirs. These include Ralitza Zaya Benazzo, Maurizio Benazzo, Lisa Breschi, and all the team at Science and Nonduality; Kent Welsh, James Haig, Tao, Kate Foley, and all at Open Circle; Don Oakley and Patty Bottari at Well Being Retreat Center; Steve and Julia Pittam, Leen, and all at Erraid and Findhorn, Johan Vellinga, IONS, MAPS, The Temple of the Way of Light, and The Chi Center. To Vera Groen and Heidi Toivonen, I appreciate you translating my work into new languages.

For my Living Impeccably and New Earth Ninja sanghas I am grateful for the spiritual friendship and community we create together. To the hundreds who have played a part in Love & Truth Party, distributing Love Letters from the Universe to thousands in dozens of countries, thank you. Special thanks to Mary Beth Davis, Chyanne Westlake, Dilhan Jayasuriya, Sunyata, Louise Croker, Tom Fortes Mayer, Georgi Johnson, Julius Dreyer, Joe Hudson, and all our guests on The TruthLover podcast (https://loveandtruthparty.pod bean.com/).

To Dilhan, Robb Drury, all who have helped organize my life and events, Ronan Attenborough, Dael Limaco, and Gaia films, my community in Melbourne, and all who supported the crowdfunding of my first book, thank you.

To the oceans, lakes, rivers, trees, flowers, sun, rain, and stars, thank you for dancing and keeping me somewhat sane. To gratitude—thank you!

References

Alexander, E. 2012. *Proof of Heaven: A Neurosurgeon's Journey into the Afterlife*. New York: Simon and Schuster.

Benson, H. 2000. *The Relaxation Response*. New York: HarperCollins.

Berman, B., and R. Lanza. 2010. *Biocentrism: How Life and Consciousness are the Keys to Understanding the True Nature of the Universe*. Dallas: BenBella Books.

Blake, W. 1956. "Letter 31." In *The Letters of William Blake,* Macmillan. https://en.wikisource.org/wiki/Page:The_letters_of_William_Blake_ (1906).djvu/205

Brown, M. 2005. *The Presence Process: A Journey into Present-Moment Awareness*. Vancouver: Namaste.

Campbell, J. 1990. *The Hero's Journey*. New York: HarperCollins.

Childre, D., and H. Martin. 2000. *The HeartMath Solution: The Institute of HeartMath's Revolutionary Program for Engaging the Power of the Heart's Intelligence*. New York: HarperOne.

Chalmers, D. 1999. "Facing Up to the Problem of Consciousness." In *The Place of Mind* (pp. 382–400), edited by Brian Cooney. Belmont, CA: Cengage Learning.

Dalai Lama. 2006. *The Universe in a Single Atom: The Convergence of Science and Spirituality*. New York: Morgan Road Books.

Daley, J. 2018. "Five Things to Know About Roger Bannister, the First Person to Break the 4-Minute Mile." *SmartNews,* https://www.smithsonianmag.com/smart-news/five-things-know-about-roger-bannister-first-person-break-four-minute-mile-180968344/.

Duhigg, C. 2012. *The Power of Habit: Why We Do What We Do in Life and Business*. New York: Random House, 2012.

Einstein, A. 1950. Letter to Dr. Robert Marcus. "The Delusion." *Letters of Note,* http://www.lettersofnote.com/2011/11/delusion.html.

Frei, P., A. H. Poulsen, C. Johansen, J. H. Olsen, M. Steding-Jessen, and J. Schüz. 2011. "Use of Mobile Phones and Risk of Brain Tumours:

Update of Danish Cohort Study." *British Medical Journal* 343, doi: https://doi.org/10.1136/bmj.d6387.

Gardner, H. 2006. *Multiple Intelligences: New Horizons in Theory and Practice*. New York: Basic Books.

Gilchrist, A. 1880. *Life of William Blake*. London: MacMillan and Co.

Goleman, D. 2005. *Emotional Intelligence*. New York: Bantam Books.

Goleman, D., and R. J. Davidson. 2017. *Altered Traits: Science Reveals How Meditation Changes Your Mind, Brain, and Body*. New York: Penguin.

Greater Good Science Center. n.d. "What Is Gratitude?" *Greater Good Magazine*. https://greatergood.berkeley.edu/topic/gratitude/definition.

HeartMath Institute. 2018. "Global Coherence Research." https://www.heartmath.org/research/global-coherence/.

Henshaw, D. L. 2011. "Mobile Phone Radiation Could Be Detected by the Human Brain." Response to Frei et al. *British Medical Journal* 343, doi: https://doi.org/10.1136/bmj.d6387.

Jung, C. 1960. *Synchronicity: An Acausal Connecting Principle*. Princeton, NJ: Princeton University Press.

Katie, B. "Do the Work." n.d. http://www.thework.com.

Keller, H. 1903. "Optimism." *Wikisource*. https://en.wikisource.org/wiki/Optimism_(Keller).

Keller, H. 1938. *Helen Keller's Journal: 1936–1937*. New York: Doubleday, Doran, and Company, Inc.

Libet, B. 1985. "Unconscious Cerebral Initiative and the Role of Conscious Will in Voluntary Action." *Behavioral and Brain Sciences* 8(4): 529–566.

Libet, B. 2003. "Can Conscious Experience Affect Brain Activity?" *Journal of Consciousness Studies* 10(12): 24–8.

Lipton, B. 2005. *The Biology of Belief: Unleashing the Power of Consciousness, Matter and Miracles*. Carlsbad, CA: Hay House.

Momoli, F., J. Siemiatycki, M. L. McBride, M. É. Parent, L. Richardson, D. Bedard, R. Platt, M. Vrijheid, E. Cardis, and D. Krewski. 2017. "Probabilistic Multiple-Bias Modeling Applied to the

Canadian Data from the Interphone Study of Mobile Phone Use and Risk of Glioma, Meningioma, Acoustic Neuroma, and Parotid Gland Tumors." *American Journal of Epidemiology* 186(7): 885–893.

Moorjani, A. 2012. *Dying to Be Me: My Journey from Cancer, to Near Death, to True Healing.* Carlsbad, CA: Hay House.

Morgen, B., Director. 2017. *Jane.* Documentary film.

Nixon, R. 1973. "Remarks at a Republican Fund-raising Dinner." *The American Presidency Project,* http://www.presidency.ucsb.edu/ws/index.php?pid=3838.

Phillips, B. 2018. "World Sub-Mile Alphabetic Register." *Track & Field News,* https://trackandfieldnews.com/stats-and-more/statistics/world-sub-4-mile-alphabetic-register/.

Pinker, S. 2018. *Enlightenment Now: The Case for Reason, Science, Humanism, and Progress.* New York: Viking.

Rosling, H. 2006. "The Best Stats You've Ever Seen." TED Talk, February 2006. http://www.ted.com/talks/hans_rosling_show_the_best_stats_you_ve_ever_seen.

Rosling, H. 2018. *Factfulness: Ten Reasons We're Wrong About the World—and Why Things Are Better Than You Think.* London: Flatiron Books.

Stapp, H. 2001. "Quantum Theory and the Role of Mind in Nature." *Foundations of Physics* 31(10): 1465–1499.

Starfield, B. 2000. "IS US Health Really the Best in the World?" *Journal of the American Medical Association* 284(4): 483–485.

Tarnas, R. 2006. *Cosmos and Psyche: Intimations of a New World View.* New York: Plume.

Tsakiris, A. 2014. *Why Science Is Wrong…About Almost Everything.* San Antonio, TX: Anomalist Books.

Turner, K. 2014. *Radical Remissions: Surviving Cancer Against All Odds.* New York: HarperOne.

van Lommel, P. 2010. *Consciousness Beyond Life: The Science of Near-Death Experience.* New York: HarperCollins.

von Neumann, J. 1932. *The Mathematical Foundations of Quantum Mechanics*. Princeton, NJ: Princeton University Press.

Wigner, E. 1967. "Remarks on the Mind Body Question, in Symmetries and Reflections, Scientific Essays." Reviewed by H. Margenau. *American Journal of Physics* 35(12): 1169–1170.

Wittgenstein, L. 1922. *Tractacus Logico-Philosophicus*. London: Kegan Paul.

World Health Organization. 2014. "Electromagnetic Fields and Public Health: Mobile Phones." October 8. http://www.who.int/news-room/fact-sheets/detail/electromagnetic-fields-and-public-health-mobile -phones.

Yehuda, R., S. M. Engel, S. R. Brand, J. Seckl, S. M. Marcus, and G. S. Berkowitz. 2005. "Transgenerational Effects of Posttraumatic Stress Disorder in Babies of Mothers Exposed to the World Trade Center Attacks During Pregnancy." *The Journal of Clinical Endocrinology & Metabolism* 90 (7): 4115–4118.

Yehuda, R., N. P. Daskalakis, L. M. Bierer, H. N. Bader, T. Klengel, F. Holsboer, and E. B. Binder. 2016. "Holocaust Exposure Induced Intergenerational Effects on FKBP5 Methylation." *Biological Psychiatry* 80 (5): 372–380.

Will Pye is a visionary entrepreneur, transformational coach, speaker, and spiritual teacher. In his early twenties, Will embarked on an intense quest exploring human potential and the nature of reality in order to overcome his own suicidal depression. He enjoyed business success while raising millions of dollars for leading charities. A series of awakenings, and then a brain tumor diagnosis in 2011, inspired a new direction. Since then, Will has given talks, meetings, workshops, and retreats—globally sharing the power of presence and gratitude for well-being and awakening. He has created life-changing online programs, including *Living Impeccably* and *A Year to Live, The Alchemy of Cancer*; and the popular podcast *The Truth Lover*.

Will is a practitioner of Zen, yoga, and Qigong, and is ever curious about integrating new-paradigm scientific research with timeless spiritual insight to facilitate true transformation and flourishing. He is founder of Love and Truth Party, a self-organizing nonprofit community and movement facilitating awakening, articulating the new paradigm, and inspiring sacred activism. Learn more at www.loveandtruthparty.org. Will divides his time between Melbourne, Australia; and Cambridge, England; and regularly travels to North America, continental Europe, South Africa, and beyond, offering meetings, workshops, and retreats. Learn more at www.willpye .com. He is author of *Blessed with a Brain Tumor*.

MORE BOOKS for the SPIRITUAL SEEKER

A SPIRITUAL GUIDE TO FREEDOM FROM
SELF-JUDGMENT & FEELINGS OF INADEQUACY

SUFFERING
IS OPTIONAL

GAIL BRENNER, PhD
FOREWORD BY RICK ARCHER

ISBN: 978-1684030156 | US $16.95

Be,
Awake,
Create

Mindful Practices to Spark Creativity

REBEKAH YOUNGER, MFA

ISBN: 978-1684032389 | US $19.95

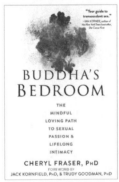

"Your guide to
transcendent sex."
—IAN KERNER, author of
the New York Times bestseller,
She Comes First

BUDDHA'S
BEDROOM

THE
MINDFUL
LOVING PATH
TO SEXUAL
PASSION &
LIFELONG
INTIMACY

CHERYL FRASER, PhD
FOREWORD BY
JACK KORNFIELD, PhD, & TRUDY GOODMAN, PhD

ISBN: 978-1684031184 | US $16.95

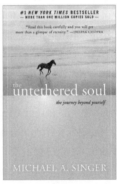

#1 NEW YORK TIMES BESTSELLER
— MORE THAN ONE MILLION COPIES SOLD —

"Read this book carefully and you will get
more than a glimpse of eternity." —DEEPAK CHOPRA

the
untethered soul

the journey beyond yourself

MICHAEL A. SINGER

ISBN: 978-1572245372 | US $16.95

new**harbinger**publications

REVEAL PRESS

Sign up *for* our spirituality e-newsletter:
newharbinger.com/join-us